A GUIDE TO
GUNUNG MULU NATIONAL PARK

A WORLD HERITAGE SITE IN SARAWAK, MALAYSIAN BORNEO

HANS P. HAZEBROEK
ABANG KASHIM BIN ABANG MORSHIDI

Edited by
K.M. WONG

Photographs and Maps by
HANS P. HAZEBROEK

Foreword by
DATO SRI ABANG HAJI ABDUL RAHMAN ZOHARI BIN TUN ABANG HAJI OPENG

Minister of Tourism, Sarawak

Natural History Publications (Borneo)
Kota Kinabalu

2002

To God Almighty, who created all this.

Published by

Natural History Publications (Borneo) Sdn. Bhd. (216807-X)
A913, 9th Floor, Phase 1, Wisma Merdeka
P.O. Box 15566, 88864 Kota Kinabalu, Sabah, Malaysia
Tel: 6088-233098 Fax: 6088-240768
e-mail: chewlun@tm.net.my
Web site: www.nhpborneo.com

First published November 2002

A Guide to Gunung Mulu National Park
A World Heritage Site in Sarawak, Malaysian Borneo
By Hans P. Hazebroek and Abang Kashim bin Abang Morshidi

ISBN 983-812-066-9

Design and layout by Hans P. Hazebroek

Front cover: Pinnacles of Gunung Api reach exceptional sizes of 45 m
    height (equivalent in height to a 15-floor building).

Endpaper (front): Deer cave is one of the world's largest known cave
    passages.

Frontispiece 1 (double page): The limestone cliffs of the Melinau
    gorge turn crimson in the light of the setting sun.

Frontispiece 2 (double page): The Pinnacles at about 1200 m altitude
    on Gunung Api.

Title page: Innumerable shades of green adorn the sea of tree crowns
    that form the canopy of Mulu's lowland forest.

Contents page: Mulu's extremely rugged limestone landscape is one of
    the world's finest examples of limestone weathering.

Facing Foreword: Bornean Treepie (*Dendrocitta occipitalis*).

Endpaper (back): The Melinau river in its broad floodplain.

Back cover: The Rhinoceros hornbill produces a dramatic whooshing
    sound of wing beats in flight.

Printed in Malaysia

Contents

Telefon: 6082-440186
Fax : 6082-444998
Email :abdurzto@sarawaknet.gov.my

KEMENTERIAN PELANCONGAN, SARAWAK
(MINISTRY OF TOURISM, SARAWAK)
TINGKAT 7, BANGUNAN MASJA,
JALAN MEDAN
93050 PETRA JAYA,
KUCHING, SARAWAK , MALAYSIA.

Menteri Pelancongan Sarawak
(Minister of Tourism, Sarawak)

FOREWORD

It gives me great pleasure to write this foreword on a book co-authored by Abang Kashim Abang Morshidi and Hans P. Hazebroek.

Indeed the authors have been known to be an authority on the subject of National Parks in Sarawak after having written a book on the subject. Throughout their professional careers they have been involved in exploring the rich biodiversity wealth of Borneo particularly that of Sarawak. One of the world's renowned national parks is the World Heritage Site of Gunung Mulu.

Gunung Mulu National Park protects some of the Earth's most entralling natural wonders. The Park's highly prominent status as a World Heritage Site accentuates its outstanding conservation values. To describe Mulu, one must invariably resort to superlatives. Mulu's impressive canyons, untamed rivers, serene rain forests, imposing mountains, spectacular limestone pinnacles and magnificent caves rank among the world's most oustanding scenery. It is impossible not to feel awed by the rain forest, by its immense riches in plants and animals, by the sense of history spanning millions of years. Unrivalled wonders of nature abound, such as the thousands of bats that spiral from the Deer Cave entrance at dusk. Gunung Api is now known to be the most cavernous mountain in the world. The pinnacles of Gunung Api, which are up to 45 metres tall, form one of the world's most dramatic limestone landscapes. Many extraordinary caves, icluding the world's largest underground chamber, the Sarawak Chamber and Deer Cave, one of the largest cave passage in the world, are within the park.

A visit to Mulu is a captivating experience, and I have no doubt that *A Guide to Gunung Mulu National Park, a World Heritage Site in Sarawak, Malaysian Borneo* will greatly enhance your enjoyment. This book is not only a superb guide book to Mulu's many attractions, but above all, a celebration of the wonders of God's creation found in the Park. Through clear explanations and illuminating photographs, the book serves to foster a deeper understanding of these natural wonders.

Mulu has become legendary for the unique accessibility of its outstanding scenery and wildlife vistas. This is the result of decades of scientific research and many years of promoting nature tourism. I am confident that this beautiful and informative book will greatly contribute to these efforts and encourage you to come and discover the wonders of Mulu for yourself.

(DATO SRI ABANG HAJI ABDUL RAHMAN ZOHARI BIN TUN ABANG HAJI OPENG)

Introducing Gunung Mulu National Park

The experience

The Gunung Mulu National Park invites you to a breathtaking experience of some of the world's most enthralling wonders of nature. The variety of attractions to enjoy and experience includes giant caves, spectacular limestone pinnacles and magnificent rain forests with vast numbers of plant and animal species. Mulu's status as a World Heritage Site underlines its outstanding conservation value.

Many spectacular caves, including the world's largest underground chamber, the Sarawak Chamber, are within the park. Some unique and beautiful caves have been equipped with lighting, pathways and plank walks to provide access: these are the "Show" caves. Deer Cave has the largest known cave passage in the world. It is estimated to house a staggering two million bats, and seeing thousands of these emerge in spiralling streams from the cave entrance at dusk is a superlative wildlife spectacle: it is witnessing one of the wonders of nature. The "Pinnacles" of Gunung Api, which are up to 45 m tall, form one of the world's most spectacular limestone landscapes. They draw attention to the hidden forces working at the rocks underlying the park, moulding the landscape.

Mulu's forests are immensely rich in plants and animals. It is estimated that the park contains at least 3500 plant species, about half of which are trees, the other half including vines and woody climbers, epiphytes, parasitic plants, palms, and herbs (Fig. 1). In addition, there are more than 8000 fungi. An astonishing 20,000 animal species, the majority of which are insects, are estimated to occur in the park. These include approximately 60 mammal species, 262 birds, 23 lizards, and 75 frogs. The park, since its establishment in 1974, has become an extremely popular destination for both local and foreign visitors.

The setting

Mulu is situated in the State of Sarawak on the great island of Borneo (Fig. 2). Sarawak, occupying the northwestern portion of Borneo, and Sabah, occupying the northern portion, are the East Malaysian states within the Federation of Malaysia. Located about 100 km east of Miri town, Mulu is the largest national park in Sarawak, with an area of 544 sq. km. The sandstone massif of Gunung (Mount) Mulu forms the highest mountain at 2376 m. There are also limestone mountains—honeycombed with caves—the highest of which are Gunung Api (1710 m) and Gunung Benarat (1615 m).

Gunung Buda—the White Mountain—is a 963-m-high limestone massif north of Gunung Mulu National Park. It houses magnificent caves, the exploration of which has only recently begun. In view of its conservation potential and its potential as a tourist destination, Gunung Buda has recently been gazetted as a national park.

The Indigenous people

The people who inhabit Sarawak's interior call themselves collectively *Orang Ulu*, upriver people. They comprise more than twenty different tribes and groups. In Mulu, the *Orang Ulu* are

Fig. 1 (Opposite). Tall riverine forest along the scenic trail to Clearwater Cave and the Cave of Winds.

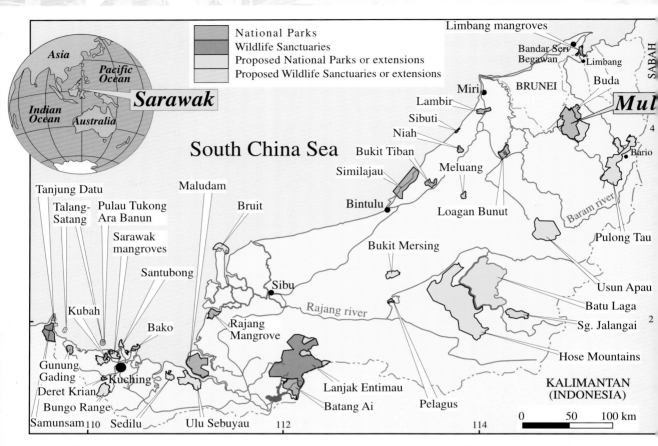

Fig. 2. Mulu's position among the proposed and existing national parks and wildlife sanctuaries of Sarawak.

represented by the Berawan, who traditionally grow hill rice and sago, and by the Penan, who traditionally were hunter-gatherers with a true nomadic life-style, but most of whom have now settled in longhouse communities. Penan elders have an unsurpassed knowledge of the rain forest. Job opportunities in and around the national park have also attracted *Orang Ulu* from other tribes, as well as people from Sarawak's coastal regions.

The World Heritage significance

Mulu's significance as a World Heritage Site becomes immediately clear from the fact that Mulu was chosen based on *all four* criteria of the World Heritage Convention, although meeting one or more criteria would have been sufficient. These criteria require that sites:

- Be outstanding examples representing major stages in earth's history, including the record of life, significant on-going geological processes in the development of land forms, or significant geomorphic or physiographical features.
- Be outstanding examples representing significant on-going ecological and biological processes in the evolution and development of terrestrial, fresh water, coastal and marine ecosystems and communities of plants and animals.
- Contain superlative natural phenomena or areas of exceptional beauty and aesthetic importance.

2

- Contain the most important and significant natural habitats for *in-situ* conservation of biological diversity, including those containing threatened species of outstanding universal value from the point of view of science of conservation.

The assessment conducted as part of the World Heritage listing procedure included the following comments:

- With its deeply-incised canyons, wild rivers, rain forest covered mountains, spectacular limestone pinnacles, cave passages and decorations, Mulu has outstanding scenic values. The natural phenomenon of millions of bats and swiftlets leaving and entering the caves is a superlative wildlife spectacle as is the less-easily appreciated life of the invertebrate world in the caves (Fig. 3).
- Mulu's caves are so long, large and complex that Gunung Api can claim to be the most cavernous mountain in the world. It is also the most studied tropical karst area in the world and it is without rival in terms of karst scenery and its setting in a mountainous rain forest.
- The giant doline of the "Garden of Eden" is a massive expression of karstic collapse whose proximity to the nearby Sarawak Chamber (the world's largest) offers one of the world's finest examples of karstic terrain.

Fig. 3. The whooshing wing roar of thousands upon thousands of bats can be heard from several kilometres distance.

Planning Your Trip

Mulu can be visited year-round, and mornings are typically clear. Any rain—more often than not—is restricted to the (late) afternoon and evening. However, it is a good idea, especially for those planning a trek, to avoid the wettest months—November to February.

How to get there

Most visitors arrive in Malaysia by air, flying into Kuala Lumpur, the capital, which is situated in Peninsular (West) Malaysia. At the Kuala Lumpur International Airport (KLIA), direct flights connect to Miri, a modern town in northern Sarawak. From Miri, travel to the park can be done in comfort by Malaysia Airlines flight. Vision Air offers flights from and to Miri and Kota Kinabalu. Since 1982, Mulu has had its own bitumen runway. Adventurous travellers can still experience the one-day journey from Kuala Baram (a settlement at the mouth of the Baram river, 20 minutes drive from Miri) by express boat and longboat up the Baram river and then up the Tutoh, a tributary of the Baram. Bookings can be made through travel agencies in Malaysia or abroad.

It is possible with a one-night stay, to see the four main show caves—fly in mid-day on the first day, fly out mid-day on the second day. However, to do justice to Mulu's great variety of breathtaking sights, a two-night stay is recommended as a minimum.

Registration, accommodation and food

The Park Headquarters has an office where all visitors must register, and a visitor centre. There is a nominal fee for entry and photo/video permits. The displays in the visitor centre are worthwhile and include pictorial explanations of selected flora and fauna as well as a large map of the park.

The Park Headquarters provides good accommodation in resthouses, chalets and in a hostel, all at reasonable prices. Tour agencies can make arrangements for any of these facilities. A canteen at the Park Headquarters provides simple meals and cold drinks. In addition, several tour agencies run their own lodges, located along the Melinau river, mostly less than 10 minutes' boat ride from the Park Headquarters. These generally provide basic but clean accommodation and excellent food. These agencies also provide transport to the park and lead tours within the park. Several modest restaurants run by local Berawan provide good food.

The Royal Mulu Resort offers superb accommodation. It is a five star hotel located on a bank of the Melinau river at 10 minutes' boat- or minibus-ride from the Park Headquarters. Rooms vary from comfortable standard rooms to luxurious suites. Bars, restaurants, a swimming pool and other facilities contribute to an outstanding quality of living.

At Camp 5, on the trail to the Pinnacles of Gunung Api, there are basic overnight facilities for a maximum of 60 persons, consisting of a hostel, roofed sleeping platforms, cooking facilities and toilets. Two Park Rangers are stationed at Camp 5. Along the trail to Gunung Mulu summit there are several camps with roofed sleeping platforms or cabins.

Equipment and clothing

The following may be useful or necessary, depending on the plan of your visit.

Fig 4 (Opposite). The Melinau Paku river along the Mulu Summit trail: pristine rain forests ensure crystal clear rivers.

CLOTHING: Shorts and T-shirts are good wear on the trails, but slacks, long-sleeved shirts and hats are recommended for protection against sunburn during boat trips. Sun block cream gives additional protection. Keep a poncho handy during boat trips and for the high camps on Mulu. Evenings and early mornings can be chilly at higher altitudes (or in a fast moving boat), and you will not regret bringing along a thin pullover.

FOOTWEAR: Trails in the forest can be very muddy after rain. In the caves, trails can also be wet and slippery. Training shoes or comfortable hiking boots with good soles are recommended. Slippers (thongs) or smooth-soled shoes are not recommended on the trails. Good footwear is essential for the climbs to the Pinnacles and the Mulu summit.

THIN SLEEPING BAG OR BLANKET: Essential for the high camps. Recommended for Camp 5 on the way to the pinnacles.

WATER BOTTLE: Essential on longer walks. Check if your tour guide is arranging drinks for you.

FOOD/COOKING EQUIPMENT: If you travel independently of a travel agent, you need to bring all food/cooking gear for overnight camps away from Park Headquarters as none is provided.

Fig 5 (Right). Gua Bulan-Susu, Moon-Milk Cave, near the highest point along the trail to Clearwater Cave/the Cave of Winds.

TORCH (FLASHLIGHT): A small, reliable torch is essential for cave visits and overnight journeys. Bring spare batteries, but do not dispose of used batteries at the campsites or in the forest. Batteries have a nasty impact on the environment. Candles are useful during overnight camps.

RUCKSACK: Essential to carry your equipment.

BINOCULARS: For birds and other wildlife; **CAMERA/FILM**

FIRST-AID KIT: For emergencies.

Drinking water

Bottled mineral water can be bought at the canteen at the Park Headquarters and at the lodges. As an alternative, boiled water can be used. Drinking from streams in the park should be avoided.

Park conservation

All animal life, plant life and non-living nature in the park is protected by law (Figs. 4–6). Visitors can make a personal contribution to conservation by avoiding to disturb any plant or animal and by avoiding to write graffiti, carving initials or otherwise vandalizing rock faces, trees or park facilities. Minimize your impact on the natural surroundings. Do not touch any dripstone structures in caves, which may have taken centuries—or even thousands of years—to form and are easily broken off or damaged. Park rules also require that rubbish be brought back to the Park Headquarters and disposed there. This is simple courtesy to other visitors. Take nothing but photographs and leave nothing but footprints! Your contribution to keep Sarawak's protected areas in pristine condition will greatly contribute to your personal enjoyment and satisfaction.

Fig 6. An unidentified shield bug displays bright colours which may warn potential predators of its distastefulness.

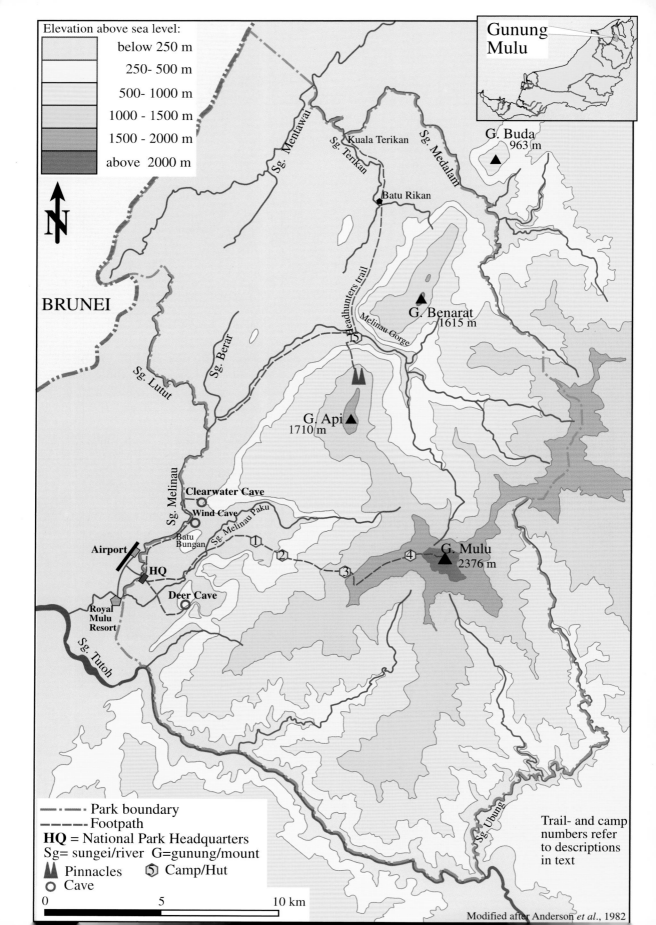

Elevation above sea level:

below 250 m

250- 500 m

500- 1000 m

1000 - 1500 m

1500 - 2000 m

above 2000 m

N

BRUNEI

Gunung Mulu

G. Buda
963 m

Sg. Mentawai

Kuala Terikan

Sg. Terikan

Sg. Medalam

Batu Rikan

Headhunters trail

Melinau Gorge

G. Benarat
1615 m

Sg. Berar

Sg. Lutut

G. Api
1710 m

Sg. Melinau

Clearwater Cave

Wind Cave

Batu
Bungan

Sg. Melinau Paku

Airport

HQ

Deer Cave

Royal
Mulu
Resort

Sg. Tutoh

G. Mulu
2376 m

Sg. Ubung

Trail- and camp
numbers refer
to descriptions
in text

Park boundary

Footpath

HQ = National Park Headquarters

Sg= sungei/river G=gunung/mount

Pinnacles   Camp/Hut

Cave

0   5   10 km

Modified after Anderson *et al.*, 1982

Exploring Mulu: Trail Guide

An excellent trail system gives access to the "Show Caves", the Pinnacles and Mulu summit, providing a first-hand experience of the rain forest along the way (Fig. 7). The "Show Caves" are those caves that have been equipped (partly or entirely) with walkways and lighting to make them safe, accessible and enjoyable. A park guide or a registered guide provided by a tour agency is required for all visitors. The trails vary from relaxing forest walks over more-or-less flat ground to fairly strenuous mountain climbs. Mulu's main trails and destinations are shown in the map on page 8, and they are also shown on the maps on pages 55 and 78 to help you recognize the main vegetation and rock types during your trek.

Historical notes on the caves

Spencer St. John, in 1862, was the first to document the existence of caves in Mulu in his well known book *Life in the Forests of the Far East*, but the local people have known the Mulu caves for generations. The name Deer Cave is derived from the deer which visited the cave to lick the salty water leaking from the guano (droppings from bats). Local Berawan people hunted the deer in this cave long before the national park was gazetted. G.E. Wilford, in the early 1960s was the first to study the geology of the more accessible caves. The first extensive exploration of the caves, however, was carried out during the Sarawak Government/Royal Geographic Society 1977/1978 Expedition. Numerous caving expeditions have since been undertaken.

Clearwater Cave

Clearwater cave can be reached either by longboat or on foot. Transport by longboat from the Park Headquarters via the Melinau river takes from 20 to 40 minutes depending on the water level of the river. The cave can also be reached from the Park Headquarters via a nature trail, involving an attractive 1.5 to 2 hours' walk.(see below).

The entrance to Clearwater Cave is 30 m up a hillside overlooking the beautiful Clearwater river, just before it joins the Melinau river. The parts of the cave which are accessible to the general public have floodlights installed. The entrance is reached via a concrete staircase of about 200 steps, and slopes down into Lady's cave. On the limestone rocks on either side of, and above the entrance grow "limestone-loving" one-leafed plants of the genus *Monophyllaea* (Fig. 8). Lady's cave has beautiful dripstone formations, including tall stalagmites, rising from the floor (Fig. 9). Further down is the underground passage of the Clearwater river itself. The passage has impressive dimensions, about 30 m high and 30 m wide. High above the river, grooves in the walls indicate previous water levels. Clearwater Cave has an extremely extensive system of passages, which is the longest known in Southeast Asia. It took many expeditions (from 1977) to survey about 107 km of the Clearwater system, but much remains to be explored.

The Nature Trail to Clearwater Cave and the Cave of Winds

Clearwater cave and the Cave of Winds can be reached from the Park Headquarters by a 3.8-km nature trail which consists partly of cement paths, partly of wooden walkways. This is a

Fig. 7 (Opposite). Trails and topography of Gunung Mulu National Park. Note that Gunung Buda, located just outside the northern park boundary, comprises a separate national park.

Fig. 8. On the dripstone above the entrance of Clearwater Cave grow single-leafed plants of the genus *Monophyllaea*.

beautiful walk that allows you to experience the rain forest first-hand. After rain, the cement and wood may become slippery due to algae and moss growths. For the first 45 minutes, starting from the Park Headquarters, the ground is flat, and the trail winds through beautiful, tall riverine forest, with occasional views of the river itself. During the rainy season the Melinau river occasionally experiences *banjir* (Malay for floods), submerging this area and depositing a fresh layer of clay and silt. Noticeable large trees along this stretch are a signposted ironwood or *belian* tree (*Eusideroxylon malagangai*) shortly beyond the Park Headquarters, and several huge strangling fig trees, easily recognized by their latticed trunks, some of which are laden with numerous large bird-nest ferns. A limestone hill, named Batu Bungan (Fig. 12) by the Penan, interrupts the floodplain and the trail climbs up via a flight of about 400 steps, partly of wood, partly of cement. Some of the attractive plants seen along this stretch of exposed limestone rocks belong to the genera *Monophyllaea*, *Amorphophallus*, and *Begonia* (see the Plant Life section below). At the highest point of the trail is Gua Bulan-susu, Moon-milk Cave. It takes only 5 minutes to pass through this cave, but it has some worthwhile features. Fig roots, some wrist-thick, others forming thin branching networks, are seen at various points inside the cave.

Dripstone formations hang beneath low ceilings and form narrow passages. Holes in the ceiling allow sparse daylight to illuminate some passages. After emerging from the cave, the trail descends via wooden stairs to the river bank clad in rich forest (Fig. 10). The trail now follows a narrow flat area between the river and the limestone hill, and twice the trail climbs up where the river flows

Fig. 9. Lady's Cave contains a wonderful array of dripstone formations, including stalagmites (foreground). **Fig. 10 (Following pages).** Ironwood staircases assist the descent of Batu Bungan into the tall riverine forest below.

Fig. 11 (Above). The King's Chamber of the Cave of Winds contains some of Mulu's most spectacular displays of dripstone formations. **Fig. 12 (Opposite).** Batu Bungan forms a precipitous limestone cliff along the Melinau river. **Fig. 13 (Following pages).** Wonderful light illuminates the Garden of Eden at the northern entrance of Deer Cave.

directly beneath the limestone rocks, allowing attractive views of the river. The Cave of Winds is reached soon after.

The Cave of Winds

From the jetty near the entrance of Clearwater cave to the entrance of the Cave of Winds, a wooden walkway leads along the steep limestone cliff above the Melinau river. The easy stroll provides good views overlooking the river and also provides close encounters with metre-long stalactites, dripstone formations hanging from the cliff face. Thereafter, the walk-way turns away from the river and up a gentle slope to the cave entrance. On the slope is limestone scree forest.

When entering the cave, you feel a cool draft, hence the name of the cave. Floodlights brighten up curved passages, narrow in places. The partly wooden walk-way passes under the bottom of a vertical shaft into which daylight falls, and eventually leads to the King's Room (Fig. 11). This is one of the most beautiful caves in Mulu and is a true wonder of nature. Stalactites hang from the ceiling and stalagmites stand on the floor in all imaginable shapes and sizes. Many are delicate and none should be touched. This underground landscape conveys the feeling of being in an entirely different world. One of the entrances of the Cave of Winds was used as a burial site between 3000 and 1500 years ago.

Fig. 14. The spectacular root system of this fig tree (*Ficus benjamina*) arches over the walkway about three quarters of the way to Deer Cave.

Deer Cave

From the Park Headquarters, a walkway (partly plank walk, partly concrete) leads to the entrance of Deer Cave. The 3-km walk takes about an hour, allowing some time to enjoy the forest and its sounds along the way. The plank walk passes through various types of rain forest: initially through lowland riverine forest which, in places, is often flooded; then through tall forest growing partly on limestone and partly on river sediments. Many trees have been labelled with both their common and scientific names. At about three-quarters of the way to Deer Cave, the walkway passes underneath the spectacular root system of a large *waringin* fig tree (*Ficus benjamina*) (Fig. 14). The ironwood or *belian* tree (*Eusideroxylon zwageri*) can also be seen in this area, where the trail follows a riverbank.

Deer cave is one of the world's largest known cave passages. It is about 2 km long and passes right through a 460-m-high limestone mountain. At the southern entrance, the concrete walkway runs beside a small stream that flows out of the cave. Upon entering, the cave opens out into a vast chamber, 120 m high and 175 m wide. The huge cave entrance allows enough daylight to enter so that these vast inside dimensions can be seen. The walkway passes initially along some rather odorous guano deposits. After rain, water drips from the ceiling. At the rear end of this chamber, the walkway winds in darkness among enormous fallen blocks, but after only a short while, the passage opens out into another huge chamber, with daylight streaming in from the northern entrance and the Garden of Eden behind (Fig. 13). A tributary of the Melinau Paku river enters the cave from the north, and disappears from view after about 300 m into a hidden passage. It emerges into daylight outside the southern entrance.

Adventurous visitors may continue, with a guide, along the river to the northern entrance. This involves scrambling over large boulders and over the flanks of a 30-m-tall guano pile as well as getting one's feet wet in the shallow river. The guano deposit lies beneath an enormous dark cavity in the ceiling of the cave. Here, a huge number (estimates reach up to 5 million) of Wrinkle-lipped bats (*Tadarida plicata*) roost during the day. The cave also houses many Mossy-nest swiftlets (*Collocalia salagana*). More details are given in the cave section on animal life below.

The flight of the bats

One of the world's natural wonders can be witnessed at the bat observatory (a clearing in front of the southern entrance to Deer Cave), on most days of reasonably dry weather. In the late afternoon, sometime around 4.30 to 6.30 p.m. (the exact time varies with the weather, and probably other unknown factors), hundreds of thousands of Wrinkle-lipped bats emerge from the cave in long spiralling streams to spend the night hunting for insects (Figs. 3, 15 & 16). On a good evening 1.8 million fly out of the cave. The whooshing roar of thousands of pairs of wings can be heard from a great distance. Sometimes a bat hawk picks out a meal from one of the bat flocks. It has been estimated that each bat eats an average of 5 g of insects a night. On a good night, the Deer Cave bat colony therefore would consume some nine tons of insects! This illustrates the importance of leaving nature unharmed. If the bat colony is destroyed for some reason, the natural balance is upset and insect plagues might result.

Fig. 15. Bats form a prolific food resource on which the Bat hawk (*Machaeramphus alcinus*) has specialized, attacking bat flocks as they exit from cave roosts during twilight.

19

Fig. 16. On a good evening 1.8 million Wrinkle-lipped bats (*Tadarida plicata*) come out from Deer Cave. Together, they may consume some nine tons of insects during the night.

Lang's Cave

A few minutes' walk from the southern entrance of Deer Cave is Lang's Cave. The cave was named in honour of the local guide who showed it to the cave explorers of the 1977/1978 expedition. This is a beautiful cave that should not be missed. It contains a wonderful array of

stalactites, stalagmites, and helictites (slender formations of mostly calcium carbonate which twist and branch in every direction on the floor, wall or ceiling). As the cave is fairly small, these features can be seen at close range. Please do not touch them as many are delicate.

The Pinnacles of Gunung Api

Gunung Api literally means "Fire Mountain". Local people have seen occasional fires on the summits of Api and nearby Benarat over the centuries. In 1929, extensive fires were observed from the coast in Brunei, about 90 km away. As the limestone is fractured, rainwater drains away

Fig. 17. In broken limestone terrain, bare limestone alternates with vegetated patches where organic matter can accumulate, allowing plants to root.

rapidly, and the peaty soil dries out during extended dry periods. Soil and vegetation may then be set on fire by lightning or even by sparks caused by falling rocks.

The Pinnacles of Gunung Api, at 1200 m altitude, form one of the world's most spectacular limestone landscapes. The view of the Pinnacles changes dramatically with the weather conditions. In clear weather, they stand out like huge white knives against the hardy trees that manage to gain foothold in narrow crevices. In wet weather, their white patina becomes dark grey on the windward side, but remains white on the lee side (Fig. 18). At this altitude, strong, chilly winds and racing clouds are common. When partly enveloped in clouds, the Pinnacles assume a mysterious character, guarding a virtually impenetrable landscape.

The route to the Pinnacles of Gunung Api is often underestimated, and requires considerable fitness. *Allow plenty of time for the return trip. Visitors have been caught by nightfall during the descent.* This adventure begins with a journey by longboat up the Melinau river. Depending on the water level in the river, visitors may be requested to help push the boat through shallow stretches. The boat trip may take up to three hours during low water levels. The Melinau river marks the park boundary. On the left is cultivated land, periodically left fallow for up to seven years before a new crop is planted. On the right is secondary forest within the park. This was cultivated one or two generations ago by the Berawans.

The boat ride is followed by a 3–4-hour walk (about 8 km) to Camp 5 on flat ground in the floodplain of the river, allowing time to enjoy the forest surroundings. The trail passes through secondary and primary lowland riverine rain forest. During the rainy season this trail can be muddy. At the start are tall bamboo clumps and trees of pioneer

Fig. 18. The knife-sharp edges of the pinnacles seen close up.

species (such as *Macaranga* spp.) on previously cultivated land. Further on, there is primary forest with magnificent stands of one of the Bornean ironwoods or *belian* (*Eusideroxylon malagangai*). Other trees that can easily be recognised are large fig trees with intertwining root systems, and huge *tapang* trees (*Koompassia excelsa*) of Leguminosae. One of the world's most spectacular flowers is native to the lowland limestone forest near Camp 5. This is *Amorphophallus cf. lambii*, a giant aroid, which grows to chest-height above the forest floor. It produces a single and much divided leaf on a tall stalk. When the leaf dies, a large flowering structure appears, also on a single tall stalk.

Camp 5, at the head of the trail leading to the Pinnacles, has wooden shelters with raised sleeping floors on a high bank of the Melinau river. Nights are often very cool here, particularly during the rainy season. Across the Melinau river from Camp 5 is a 400-m-high, vertical limestone cliff. This is the southwest face of Gunung Benarat. The entrance to Tiger cave is high up the cliff. The Melinau river flows between the Api and Benarat mountains through the Melinau Gorge. A suspension bridge across the Melinau river connects to the Headhunters' Trail (see below). After spending the night in Camp 5, the ascent follows the lower slopes of Gunung Api to the Pinnacles at 1200 m altitude. The horizontal distance to the Pinnacles is about 2 km, but the gain in altitude is well over 1000 m. Depending on one's fitness, this tough walk can take anywhere between two-and-a-half to four-and-a-half hours or longer. The first part of about 750 m climb upwards, is a steep walk through limestone forest. The last 300 m up is a scramble over limestone rock with sparse vegetation. Aluminum ladders have been fixed over the steepest stretches. The return trip takes about the same time, as the very sharp and broken limestone makes movement, either up or down, slow and hazardous. A fall on these sharp rocks is likely to cause considerable injury and is potentially lethal. It is important to start off early, and to keep an eye on the time.

The Headhunters' Trail

This journey offers a superb way to experience Mulu's rain forests, including jungle trekking and river travel, with the additional appeal an overnight stay at an Iban longhouse. The Headhunters' Trail follows part of an ancient route taken by Kayan headhunting parties who paddled up the Melinau River to the beginning of the Melinau Gorge. From there they dragged their longboats across the watershed to the Terikan River, a distance of about 3 km through the forest. After paddling down the Terikan River, they dispatched headhunting parties to raid longhouses in the Limbang area. Several tour operators organise the trek and since the journey includes an overnight stay at Camp 5, the option of climbing to the Pinnacles is usually part of the package.

The Headhunters' Trail trek can be done either way, beginning or ending in Limbang. If the journey begins at Mulu Park Headquarters, the route to Camp 5 (described above under "The Pinnacles of Gunung Api") is initially followed. The journey continues at the suspension bridge across the Melinau river. From here the trail to Kuala Terikan is over flat ground, briefly through lowland limestone forest, but mainly through beautiful riverine forest, and takes about 4–5 hours (11.3 km) allowing for time to enjoy the forest scenery along the way. The night can be spent in basic accommodation at the ranger station of Nanga Mentawai, about 15 minutes' walk from Kuala Terikan. Alternatively, if time permits, the trip can be continued on the same day by longboat to reach the longhouse Rumah Bala Lesong for an overnight stay. The boat trip takes 3–4 hours, depending on the water level and on the power of the outboard engine. Resuming the downriver journey the next day, Nanga Medamit is reached. From there, the journey is by road to Limbang Town.

Gunung Mulu Summit

Unlike Gunung Api, Gunung Mulu is largely a sandstone and shale mountain, rather than limestone. The long uphill walk to Gunung Mulu's summit (2376 m) begins at an altitude of about 20 m above sea level. The return trip from the Park Headquarters can be comfortably done in five days, assuming good physical fitness. The suggested schedule below allows time to observe and enjoy the interesting and beautiful sights along the way. Obviously this schedule needs be tailored to your specific interests and abilities. Above Camp 3 (1270 m) the walk may be quite strenuous as there are some steep stretches that must be negotiated by holding onto roots and small trees. Near the summit there is a particularly steep stretch. Ropes have been fixed there to aid the ascent. Tents are not necessary as simple wooden shelters (providing sleeping floors) are available.

Fig. 19. Crystal clear water of the Melinau Paku river forms a welcome refreshment along the Mulu Summit trail.

The interesting walk to Camp 1 at 150 m altitude can be done in three to four hours on the *first day*. The trail passes initially through lowland riverine forest with frequently flooded areas, and occasional limestone outcrops (Fig. 19). After rain, this flat part of the trail can be very muddy. Beautiful ground orchids are sometimes seen blooming along the path and wild durian trees may be fruiting. There are two river crossings (without bridges), but unless it has rained heavily, the water is only knee-deep. The path then gradually rises through mainly tall mixed dipterocarp forest. Along the way are interesting trees, such as dipterocarps with large buttresses, and enormous fig trees. Ask your guide to point out a particularly large fig tree which is hollow—the host tree that it used as a support had died long ago. The host has been entirely decomposed by fungi, termites and other organisms. You can enter the centre of this hollow fig tree and look up into the 25-m-high tunnel in which the host once grew (Fig. 22). This may help to appreciate the life history of large rain forest trees, which may span many human lifetimes. After crossing the knee-deep Nyipa river, a small but turbulent tributary of the Melinau Paku, the trail goes uphill following the river bank to Camp 1, which has a wooden shelter. The boulders in the river are of sandstone from the Mulu Formation. An old helicopter pad with young secondary vegetation near the camp is a good bird-watching location.

On the *second day* is the long uphill walk to Camp 3 at 1270 m (Camp 2 does not have a shelter). Up to about 800 m elevation is magnificent tall mixed dipterocarp forest. A conspicuous

Fig. 20 (Below). Camp 3, the second highest shelter on Gunung Mulu.

Fig. 21 (Left). This *Eria robusta* orchid grows near the ground, sheltered from the wind by hardy shrubs in the dense vegetation of Gunung Mulu's summit region.

Fig. 22 (Opposite). You can look up through a cylindrical weavework of roots within the hollow centre of this enormous fig tree (*Ficus* sp.). The inside of the basket is about 2.5 m across—a space once occupied by the tree that provided support for the fig during its earlier growth.

and common dipterocarp along the ridge trail is *kapur bukit* (*Dryobalanops beccarii*), which has yellowish-ochre to red-brown flaky bark and reaches gigantic dimensions. Above 800 m there is a gradual transition to montane forest. The chorus of cicadas diminishes imperceptibly at first, but soon the relative silence of the montane forest makes the occasional bird song stand out. At around 1200 m, the air is notably cooler and rocks, tree trunks and branches are covered in mosses. The trees are shorter and more light reaches the forest floor, encouraging a herb layer. The trail becomes fairly steep, leading through mossy forest. Frequent cloud development on the mountain from this level upward soaks the forest in moisture. Camp 3 is in a small clearing in this forest. It has a spacious wooden shelter with rainwater tanks for drinking and washing (Fig. 20).

On the *third day,* the journey continues to camp 4 at 1800 m. For the first one to two hours, the trail is fairly steep until at 1600 m, when the crest of the west ridge is reached. The path along the west ridge is over strongly undulating terrain with mossy forest (Fig. 24). Overall, the gain in altitude along the ridge is only about 200 m, but this walk is quite strenuous due to the many fairly steep, short ascents and descents. In the low parts there are swampy patches. On the exposed crests, pitcher plants hang down from the branches and rhododendrons grow between the trees. One of the swampy patches along the west ridge is called "Rhino Lake". It is reputed to be here, before the Second World War, that one of the last rhinoceroses was shot and then tracked to a small summit 10 km north of the main Mulu summit, where it died. This summit, on the northern park boundary, is called Gunung Tamacu (Rhinoceros Mountain). Camp 4 is on the west ridge, in a

Fig. 23 (Below). A Bornean mountain ground squirrel (*Dremomys everetti*) forages in the undergrowth of the mossy forest at about 1800 m elevation on Gunung Mulu.

Fig. 24 (Right). Dense mossy forest encloses the path along the west ridge of Gunung Mulu at about 1650 m elevation.

Fig. 25 (Opposite). The pitcher plant *Nepenthes muluensis* is confined to only a few mountains in northern Sarawak.

small clearing in the mossy forest, at 1800 m elevation (Fig. 23). It has a wooden shelter and rainwater tanks. Nights are cold at this elevation, particularly during wet weather and a sleeping bag is essential. Weather permitting, the best view is from a helicopter pad about 50 m from the camp (Fig. 26). The valley of the Melinau river, as well as Gunung Api and Gunung Benarat, can be seen from here. Your best chance to get a clear view is just after sunrise, 6.00 to 6.30 a.m. Soon afterwards, clouds may envelop the mountains.

On the *fourth day*, a steep section remains, leading to the summit at 2376 m. Ropes have been fixed over the steepest, most hazardous stretches just below the summit. Be careful, particularly on the way back. The stretch from Camp 4 to the summit may take from one-and-a-half to three

hours. In clear weather, the summit view is splendid, but clouds often obscure the view by the time the summit is reached. Plant life of the summit area is both interesting and beautiful (Figs. 21 & 25). It consists of shrubs, at most one metre high, dominated by rhododendrons. The pitcher plant, *Nepenthes muluensis*, suspends its purple-streaked pitchers in masses from the top branches of the rhododendrons. The only other location where it has been collected is Gunung Murud. Subtly beautiful orchids grow among the shrubs. The return trip from the summit to Camp 3 may take about 6 to 7 hours. Allow enough time to reach Camp 3 in daylight. From Camp 3 the Park Headquarters can be reached in one day.

Adventure caving

As a result of many caving expeditions since 1977, a total of about 286 km of passages were surveyed for all Mulu's caves taken together. This is thought to be less than half of the total extent of all the caves in Mulu. For those with stamina and who are willing to spend longer periods underground in caves without facilities such as pathways and lighting, there is much to be explored. Most of these trips require at least some ability to climb and to swim. The discomfort of getting wet, dirty and tired is all part of the game. But the rewards include impressive and beautiful sights.

Fig. 26. Clouds roll in soon after dawn, enshrouding Mulu's summit.

For safety reasons, all adventure cavers must be accompanied by a registered park guide. Usually three to four hours are spent in each cave. Your itinerary will depend on the time available for the trip, the availability of a competent park guide, the weather conditions, and the fitness of the participants. For safety reasons, group size is restricted to a maximum of six participants. The park ranger will advise you on the most suitable itinerary. Locations for adventure caving include caves of various difficulty (up to Grade 5): Benarat Caverns, Clearwater/Snake track, Cobra, Deer Water, Drunken Forest, Lagang, Link/Clearwater, Sarawak Chamber, Porcupine, Snake, and Wind Caves.

Caving equipment is not supplied by the park. Adventure cavers must bring their own equipment, such as helmets and Single Rope Technique (SRT) equipment where appropriate for their caving plan. The use of carbide is no longer allowed in the park. For adventure caving, it is wise to make reservations in advance with the National Parks and Wildlife office, Forest Department, Miri (Tel: 6085-436637, Fax: 6085-417629). Research and exploration of the caves or forests require permission from the Sarawak State Government in Kuching.

In the Rain Forest

The initial impression many people get, when stepping into a rain forest for the first time, is an intense feeling of being overwhelmed by the enormous variety of life forms. The subdued light levels under the canopy; the countless different shapes and colours of leaves, tree trunks, herbs and climbers; the awesome blend of unidentified sounds; and the variety of mysterious scents all contribute to your sense of wonder and your desire to discover things never seen before. Give yourself some time to tune in to some of the wonders of this new world.

Years of study by scores of specialists have shown that Gunung Mulu National Park is of great ecological significance because it contains all of the major vegetation types of Sarawak with the exception of those derived on igneous rocks. Mulu's vegetation types represent an unusually rich variety of habitats (or local environments), each of which provides the living requirements for its own assemblage of plants and animals. Thus, there is an enormous diversity of plants and animals within the park. Many of the species found at the park are either endemic to Borneo or even to specific areas of the park: this means that these species are found nowhere else in the world! Despite the many studies carried out so far, only a limited number of the total species numbers have been described—particularly for insects, fungi and micro-organisms.

Underlying Mulu's rich variety of habitats are the dramatic variations in the local geology and topography. Each rock type is associated with a specific group of soils. Each altitudinal range is associated with its own climatic variations. Climate, rocks, soils, plants and animals interact over time and must be considered as part of an integrated entity.

ANIMAL LIFE

Animal diversity

An astonishing 20,000 animal species, the majority of which are insects, are estimated to occur in the park. Approximately 60 species of mammals, 262 birds, 23 lizards, and 75 frogs have been recorded. Fourteen frog species were new records for Borneo. Among insects, at least 5000 beetles occur in the park, and there are also 360 spiders, 276 butterflies, 2400 moths (out of an estimated total of 3000 to 4000 for the whole of Borneo), and 72 termite species.

Rarity of animals

Animals such as birds and insects are readily heard or seen. But despite the immense diversity of animals in the park, the larger animals are not conspicuous in the rain forest. Population densities are generally low and the larger animals are shy. Many animals are well camouflaged, many live in the tree crowns high overhead, and many are only active at night. However, with the help of a park guide, patience, quiet conduct and some background knowledge of animal's habits, you have an excellent chance to see some of Mulu's shy animals.

Forest richness and niches

The riverine and lowland mixed dipterocarp forests provide the living space for most of the animals. Here, where plant life is richest, the animal life also reaches its greatest diversity. In the specialised forests on poorer soils, i.e., the *kerangas* and lowland limestone forests, overall animal

---

Fig. 27 (Opposite). The Plain pigmy squirrel (*Exilisciurus exilis*) has a length of only about 12 cm, including the tail. It forages on the bark of trees and lianas, feeding on various small insects. It is confined to Borneo.

33

diversity is distinctly reduced. Plants on these poorer soils tend to have less digestible plant parts such as leaves that stops them from being eaten and this is advantageous since replacing them is difficult if nutrients are scarce. Also in the montane forest, the overall diversity of the animal life is much reduced. Among many reasons, this reduction may be due to the smaller number of fruit tree species in specialised forests which results in a smaller number of niches. However, there are certain specialist insect groups, particularly among the moths (e.g., the subfamily Larentiinae of the family Geometridae), that have their greatest diversity in montane forest.

The niche of a species has been likened to its functional position or profession, and this is a useful way to understand the term. By having a slightly different niche, a species can exist and co-exist with other species that otherwise have similar niches, and so avoids competing for the same resources, such as food and shelter. A good example, as shown by study in Indonesian Borneo, is the co-existence of as many as seven species of hornbills in the same forest. Two are nomadic, the Wreathed and Wrinkled hornbills, travelling in flocks over large distances between different parts of the forest where fat-rich fruits are abundant. They keep track of specific fruiting seasons, but use a lot of energy in the process. Two species, the Rhinoceros and Helmeted hornbills, have breeding pairs that each occupy a territory. But although breeding adults are territorial, flocks of up to eight juveniles, subadults, and non-breeding adults are nomadic. Three species, the White-crested, Bushy-crested and Black hornbills, live in groups that also have their own territory each. All five territorial (or partly territorial) species save energy by staying within fixed areas. When the preferred trees with fat-rich fruits in their area are not fruiting, they supplement their diets with sugary figs and small animals. In Mulu, all eight species of hornbills known in Borneo have been recorded.

Mammals

It is reputed that the last rhinoceros in Mulu was hunted and killed just before the Second World War. Once in the past, these magnificent animals may have been quite common in Mulu. As indicated by Berawan guides, large pools on some ridges of Gunung Mulu presumably represent their wallows. Short, deeply worn sections of their trails still seem to remain visible in a few places. Wild cattle or *tembadau* (*Bos javanicus*) became extinct in Sarawak in the first half of this century. According to Berawan eye-witnesses, small herds roamed the forests near the Melinau river in Mulu until the 1940s.

The Bearded pig (*Sus barbatus*) is probably the most common large mammal in the park (Fig. 28). Traces of pigs are occasionally seen along the trails, where they have dug up the soil in search of tubers or worms. Their preferred food, however, consists of fruits and seeds. They are particularly fond of acorns, and when the oaks in the lower montane forest are fruiting, you may be able to catch a glimpse of Bearded pigs along the Mulu summit trail. The pigs also relish dipterocarp fruits, some of which can contain up to 70% fat.

Bearded pigs are often close-ranging, but sometimes they roam widely, occasionally in large herds. People living in the headwaters of Sarawak's major rivers report that in certain months, there are no pigs around, and in other months they are extremely abundant, suggesting irregular, somewhat unpredictable but very definite migrations of different scales. This phenomenon of bearded pig migration was studied in 1983. Large herds of up to 100 or more bearded pigs were documented to have travelled considerable distances in that year, in response to a major fruiting of the dipterocarps. From export data of *engkabang* nuts (the local name for certain fat-rich

---

Fig. 28 (Opposite above). Bearded pigs (*Sus barbatus*) forage occasionally during the day, but are mostly active at night. Their diet includes fallen fruits and seeds, roots, herbs, earthworms and other small animals.
Fig. 29 (Opposite below). Long-tailed macaques (*Macaca fascicularis*) eat many kinds of food, including fruits, seeds, leaves and small animals.

dipterocarp fruits) it appeared that the dipterocarps had been fruiting abundantly for four consecutive years: 1980–1983. This was unusual, as the fruiting seasons of many dipterocarps are generally very irregular and mostly several years apart. Fruit crops within one fruiting season are not fully synchronised between different areas, and so the pigs move from one fruit crop to another. There was also a bumper crop of sugary, non-dipterocarp fruits, such as wild figs, in 1983. These unusual fruiting patterns were presumably related to the 1982–1983 El Niño weather event which caused drought in much of Southeast Asia.

The abundance of dipterocarp fruits during four consecutive years, followed by a sugary fruit bumper crop, is thought to have resulted in a dramatic increase in the pig population. In times of food abundance, newborn piglets mature quickly, and reproduce within a year. Large herds were seen to cross rivers, and were hunted relentlessly. Based on interviews with hunters from many longhouses in the basin of the upper Baram river, major migration paths could be reconstructed. Written records of local schools that bought wild boar meat, provided an independent check on the accounts of hunters, and gave a close match. The total number of wild pig migrating during 1983 in the upper Baram area may have been as much as 800,000.

Three kinds of deer occur in the park, and all are wary. The most likely time to see any of them along the forest trails is at night with a flash light. The largest are the Sambar deer or *rusa* (*Cervus unicolor*). They are dark reddish-brown and when mature, have a shoulder height of about 120 cm. Of smaller size are the barking deer or *kijang* (*Muntiacus* spp.), with two species in Borneo. Their loud "barking" is unmistakable and sounds like a dog barking frantically. Two species of mouse deer occur in the park, the *napu* or Greater (*Tragulus napu*) and *pelanduk* or Lesser (*T. javanicus*). They are not true deer, but belong to a separate family (Tragulidae) with only four species in Africa and East Asia. These are the world's smallest hoofed animals, with a head-and-body length of some 55 cm (the *napu*) and 45 cm (the *pelanduk*). They feed mainly on fruit and young leaves. In the field their most striking features, apart from their small size, are the large eyes and the white underside of the tail (which is clearly visible when a mouse deer bounds off).

There is no historical record of Orang-utans (*Pongo pygmaeus*) in the Mulu region. However, abundant Orang-utan remains were found in cave deposits at Niah, which is far outside their present distribution. This indicates that the Orang-utan once had a much wider distribution through Borneo and therefore it may well have roamed in Mulu.

Like Orang-utans, Bornean gibbons (*Hylobates muelleri*) are tail-less primates or apes. Their melancholy calls in the early morning are among the most magnificent sounds of the rain forest. These calls mark their territories, and can be heard over a great distance. They feed mainly on fruits and young leaves, but eat also flowers and insects. When travelling, gibbons swing by their long arms along the branches, reaching amazing speeds. During the 1977/1978 expedition, their calls were among the more familiar sounds in the Mulu forests. They have been sighted as high as 1600 m elevation in the mossy forest on Gunung Mulu. Their loud calls mean that they are extremely easy to find by hunters, and their monogamous, territorial habit means that hunting one animal disrupts breeding and social patterns of an entire group.

Four species of monkeys are known from Mulu and each occupies its own niche. They can co-exist by eating different food, by spending most of their time at different levels in the canopy or by selecting different times to search for food. Monkeys and apes play an essential role in the dispersal of many plant species. Many seeds are eaten with the fruit, surviving in the primates' digestive tracts and germinate in a different place in the forest after being expelled in their droppings. The Long-tailed macaque (*Macaca fascicularis*) and Pig-tailed macaque (*M. nemestrina*) are probably the most widespread (Fig. 29). They live in large groups and eat a variety of food, but mostly fruit. The Pig-tailed macaques spend relatively more time on or near the forest floor.

The Red leaf monkey (*Presbytis rubicunda*) and Hose's leaf monkey (*P. hosei*) eat mostly seeds and young leaves. Red leaf monkeys appears to find their food mainly in small understorey trees and lianas. This is because the leaves of the dipterocarp trees that dominate the canopy are indigestible. Leaf monkeys or langurs form small groups of rarely more than six individuals. Of the two species, the Red leaf monkey is perhaps the more likely to be encountered. Small groups are sometimes spotted along the trail to the Pinnacles of Gunung Api.

The world's smallest bear, the Sun bear (*Helarctos malayanus*) is also a resident in Mulu, but it is rarely seen. Traces of its presence can be seen on tree trunks that are pitted and scarred where its sharp, curved claws have gripped to climb to bees' nests. A gaping hole lined with shreds of bark and splinters of wood would be left behind where a bees' nest had been in a cavity within the trunk. Such scars leave little doubt about the considerable force used to rip open the tree and get to the honey.

Civets and mongooses (family Viverridae) form a diverse group of carnivores, most of which have slender cat-like bodies and a long tail. Their muzzles are unlike a cat's, being rather pointed and long. Civets are mainly active at night, while mongooses forage during the day. The mongooses' tapering tail, with hair longer near the base than at the tip, is a good field character. Twelve species of civets and mongooses occur in Borneo.

During the 1977/1978 expedition, two male *tangalung* or Malay civets (*Viverra tangalunga*) were caught in snares, fitted with radio collars and released. One of the civets was not found again, but the remaining animal could be tracked. The civet was tracked at night, and followed on foot with a portable antenna. In the forest, the signals transmitted by the radio collar had a maximum tracking range of 1 km. The civet's movements were watched using red light, which did not seem to disturb it. This technique allowed the researchers to watch the civet for two months. The civet travelled alone at night through a home range of less than one sq. km of lowland riverine forest. This range was bounded by limestone outcrops and streams. During the day the civet rested in small caves or dense undergrowth, but during rainstorms it sheltered up trees. At night the civet was seen to catch frogs and grasshoppers and also eat carrion and fruit (Fig. 30). It used several

Fig. 30. The Malay civet (*Viverra tangalunga*) roams the forest at night. Its diet includes a variety of small animals but also fruits, taken mainly from the forest floor.

capture techniques. It paused, appeared to listen, then plunged its head into the undergrowth. Or it would pause, appear to listen, then run and grab its prey. Or it would sit down, sniff up and down a tall plant for a while, then snap at small prey, or move on. During watches when detailed capture rates were noted, the civet appeared to have an amazing success rate with an average of one prey item every two minutes. In most cases it could not be seen what prey exactly the civet was catching. Therefore, droppings of the civet were analysed for recognisable animal bones or vegetation. It appeared that cave swiftlets, bats, beetles, leaves, and fruits were all part of its diet.

The Malay weasel (*Mustela nudipes*) is also known from Mulu, where it has been seen active during the day. It also forages at night and feeds on small animals. It has surprisingly bright colours with an orange body and whitish head. It sleeps in holes in the ground. In the mountain forests of Gunung Mulu live Bornean mountain ground squirrels (*Dremomys everetti*). They can be recognised by their short, bushy tail and somewhat pointed head (Fig. 23). They forage in the undergrowth, looking for insects, earthworms and fruits.

One of the tiniest mammals in the world is Savi's pigmy shrew (*Suncus etruscus*). It has a head-and-body length of about 5 cm. It catches insects on the ground in Mulu's tall dipterocarp forests. Another remarkable insect eater is the Moonrat (*Echinosorex gymnurus*). Its name is misleading as it does not belong to the rats, which are rodents, but is grouped together with the shrews in the order Insectivora. It is some 35 cm long (without the tail) and almost totally white, and so it is easily picked up in the beam of a flashlight. Its pungent, ammonia-like smell and its conspicuous appearance may serve to warn predators that it is inedible. Other interesting mammals in Mulu include the Western tarsier, flying lemur, and the Slow loris.

The occurence of the Orange tube-nosed bat (*Murina cyclotis*) was only recorded for Borneo during the 1977/1978 expedition. These bats have pale orange or grey fur and nostrils which are expanded into short tubes. They hunt insects in the understorey of lowland forest and are not known to roost in caves. The discovery brings the number of bat species known from the park to a staggering twenty-seven.

Bird Watching

Because of the great range in altitudes and vegetation types, Mulu's bird fauna is very rich, with 262 recorded species (Figs. 32–38). The cooler, moister mountain forests support a smaller and less diverse bird fauna than the lowland forests. On Gunung Mulu there is a progressive reduction in bird species with elevation, from 171 species in the lowland rain forest to only about 12 in the upper montane forest at about 1300 m. Birds play an essential role in the dispersal of many plant species.

All eight hornbill species known in Borneo have been recorded in Mulu. The spectacular White-crested hornbill (*Berenicornis comatus*) lives in groups and magnificent flocks of five or more are sometimes seen overhead when traversing rivers along the Mulu summit trail. Their flight is almost silent, unlike that of other large hornbill species. Adults have a beautiful white crest, white wing tips and white tail. They feed probably mainly on small animals such as lizards and small birds but also on many species of fruit. When looking for food, they hop and climb through a tree crown, digging among epiphytes, prising off bark and splitting husks of capsules. Natural holes in trees are selected for breeding, where the female imprisons herself by narrowing the entrance with earth, helped by the male. Usually a single chick is raised and fed by all older members of a group. They do not breed every year. These nesting habits are common to all Bornean hornbills. White-crested hornbills form resident groups of usually four to six birds that occupy a territory of about 1.6 sq. km.

Fig. 31 (Opposite). The Plantain squirrel (*Callosciurus notatus*) is mostly active during the early morning and late afternoon. It feeds on a wide variety of fruits and insects, mostly ants.

Fig. 32 (Top left). The Thick-billed spiderhunter (*Arachnotera crassirostris*) is a scarce bird of lowland forests. It feeds on nectar of flowers but is also insectivorous. Spiderhunter nests are sewn to the underside of large leaves with spider-web threads piercing the leaf for attachment. **Fig. 33 (Top right).** This mountain Imperial pigeon (*Ducula badia*) breeds in the montane forests of Gunung Mulu. However, these birds make daily flights to lowland feeding areas. **Fig. 34 (Above).** Chick of a Jambu fruit-dove (*Ptilinopus jambu*) on the nest. The adult takes fruit from trees and also fruit fallen on the ground. **Fig. 35 (Opposite).** The Rhinoceros hornbill produces a dramatic whooshing sound of wing beats in flight.

Fig. 36 (Right). Jungle babblers are inconspicuous, rather quiet birds living on or close to the ground in thickets. Sometimes they work up vine-covered trees hunting insects. They build cup-shaped nests in trees and bushes.

Fig. 37 (Below). Bornean treepies (*Dendrocitta occipitalis*) feed on a mixed diet of fruit and insects in Mulu's mountain forest, uttering bell-like, three-note whistles.

Fig. 38 (Opposite). This Rhinoceros hornbill (*Buceros rhinoceros*) is feeding on ripe figs.

Population densities of other large hornbills in the lowland forests of Sarawak are very low, with only one resident Rhinoceros hornbill pair (*Buceros rhinoceros*) recorded per 1.2 sq. km of forest (Fig. 35 & 38). Although breeding adults of the Rhinoceros hornbill and Helmeted hornbill (*Buceros vigil*) are territorial, juveniles, subadults, and non-breeding adults travel far between fruit crops. Such nomadic hornbills are known to have home ranges as large as 300 sq. km. Thus huge tracts of forest need to be preserved to protect viable populations of the nomadic hornbills. Hornbills depend on nest sites in large, hollow older trees and may therefore be unable to breed successfully in production forests, where trees are harvested at or before maturity. Some species, particularly the spectacular Rhinoceros and Helmeted hornbills, are widely hunted for the decorative quality of their feathers, casque and meat although all eight species are totally protected by law in Sarawak.

Trogons are among the most beautiful birds of Mulu's rain forest. They are brightly coloured with a short, broad bill and a long, square-cut tail, which makes them easy to recognise. The underside of the tail is whitish. They usually perch in the shady understorey of the forest, and sit upright on a horizontal branch on the look-out for insects. Six species occur in Borneo. The Scarlet-rumped trogon (*Harpactes duveaucelii*) is a jewel that may sometimes be seen in the lowland forest along the plank walk to Deer Cave. Its bill is vividly cobalt blue, as is the skin

around its eye. The male's belly and rump are brilliantly red, but the female's are pink. The voice of the male is a very soft series of descending notes.

In the montane forests of Gunung Mulu, Bornean treepies (*Dendrocitta occipitalis*) feed on a mixture of fruit and animal material. They search for small animals by working their way steadily through the canopy, pausing while looking for prey (Fig. 37).

Borneo has 11 kingfisher species. Some live along rivers and catch fish, but others live in the forest, away from water, where they nest in tree trunks and feed on insects. The largest of them all is often seen during boat rides on the Melinau river. This is the Stork-billed kingfisher (*Pelargopsis capensis*), which has a very long red bill. When it flies low above the water, the silky light blue of the lower back and rump reflect the bright sunlight. It sits on dead branches overlooking the water and makes spectacular dives to catch fish. It has a very loud voice, and flies off with a sharp, laughing cry when disturbed.

Reptiles and amphibians

Borneo's snake fauna is the richest in Southeast Asia, with at least 154 species belonging to 64 genera in 10 families. Five species are vipers, easily recognised from the triangular shape of the head. This is a group of venomous snakes, but the effect of their venom to humans is usually confined to pain and swelling in the region of the bite. Dangerous symptoms are rare but do occur. The Bornean vipers have a pit on each side of the head, between eye and nostril. This pit is a heat-sensitive organ that enables the snake to detect warm-blooded animals even at night. Pit vipers often remain virtually motionless for several days. They rely on their excellent camouflage to remain unseen.

Occasionally seen along trails in Mulu's lowland forests, the Sumatran pit viper (*Trimeresurus sumatranus*) grows to a length of about one metre. It is pale green in colour, with subtle darker green bands at 2 to 4 cm intervals, and the tip of the tail is reddish. Its fangs may be over a

Fig. 39 (Above). Growing to a length of at most 50 cm, the Painted mock viper (*Psammodynastes pictus*) is very mildly venomous but presents no danger to humans because its fangs are at the back of its mouth. These little snakes are also called mock vipers. **Fig. 40 (Opposite Above).** Sumatran pit vipers (*Trimeresurus sumatranus*) hunt rodents, birds, and other small prey. They may remain in the same place for days on end, waiting for such prey to approach. **Fig. 41 (Opposite Below).** Swamp frogs (*Rana baramica*) call from low vantage points in riverine forest. Adults feed on cockroaches and other small insects.

Fig. 42 (Left). Huntsman spiders do not build orb webs, but pursue their prey on foliage or bark surfaces.

Fig. 43 (Below). This huntsman spider carries its egg sack under its body.

centimetre long. Curled up on the branch of a low tree, it waits for a rodent, bird, or other small prey to come close, then moves like lightning to catch it (Fig. 40). At most 50 cm in length, the Painted mock viper (*Psammodynastes pictus*) has a subtle brown-yellow pattern. It does not belong to the viper family but to the water snakes (Subfamily Homalopsinae). Only mildly venomous, they present no danger to humans because their fangs are at the back of the mouth. These small snakes are not easily frightened, which has earned them the name of mock vipers (Fig. 39). Two species occur in Borneo.

The distribution of Mulu's presently known 75 species of frogs is strongly related to different types of environment. In flooded *kerangas* forests and in peatswamp forests, the water is clear but tea-coloured due to humic acids. Here live specialist frogs that are adapted to the acid water. Different species behave and find their food in different ways, which allows them to co-exist in the same environment. Here, the Swamp frog (*Rana baramica*) calls from stumps or forks in the trunks of small trees and vines, about 1–2 m above the ground. It has prominent, golden eyes, a large eardrum, and long fingers and toes (Fig. 41). Adults eat cockroaches and other small insects.

Fig. 44 (Opposite). Green tree lizards (*Bronchocoela cristatella*) frequent open patches in the rain forest. They are agile hunters and capable of catching dragonflies on the wing.

Insects

The Bornean butterfly fauna is extremely rich and is estimated to include approximately 900 species. Of these, 276 were recorded during the 1977/1978 expedition. The cooler, moister montane forests support a smaller and less diverse butterfly fauna as compared to the lowlands. Butterflies on Gunung Mulu decrease in diversity upwards and especially towards the montane forest. In the montane forest, upwards from about 1000 m, there is a distinctive butterfly fauna. This montane butterfly fauna is more numerous on the Gunung Api limestone mountain than on the sandstone and shale of Gunung Mulu itself. Butterflies may play an important role in the pollination of Bornean orchids, as indicated by pollen found on collected specimens. Holloway observed migration of butterflies whereby, within two hours, some hundred *Saletara liberia* individuals, often two or three together, passed over the south ridge of Gunung Mulu at 1800 m elevation. These are handsome butterflies of the family Pieridae. They are medium-sized (about 5 cm wingspan) and largely white.

One of the most spectacular butterflies is Rajah Brooke's birdwing (*Trogonoptera brookiana brookiana*). It was first described by Wallace in 1855. It has emerald green, feather-like markings on the velvety black forewings, and a red collar behind the head (Fig. 45). The wing span of 15 to 17 cm is huge for a butterfly. The male is not uncommon along the banks of streams in lowland forest, and several together may settle on patches of ground moistened by urine. The much rarer female flies mostly higher, and is sometimes seen 10 m or higher above the ground around flowering trees. The beautiful bright orange flowers of the small *Ixora* tree form a special attraction for Rajah Brooke's, and other birdwing butterflies (Fig. 46). This tree is not uncommon in the

Fig. 45 (Below). Rajah Brooke's birdwing butterfly (*Trogonoptera brookiana brookiana*) has a huge wing span of up to 17 cm. Males are sometimes seen sipping moisture along the banks of streams in lowland forest.

Fig. 46 (Above). The flowers of the small tree *Ixora* sp. attract birdwing butterflies.

Fig. 47. This moth (*Eumelea biflavata*) displays bright colours which may warn potential predators that it is distasteful or poisonous.

Fig. 48 (Above). Fiddle beetles (*Mormolyce* sp.) scavenge among the leaf litter in search of food, which often includes other smaller insects. Their name derives from the highly flattened body and extremely elongated head, together resembling the shape of a violin. When attacked by predators, these beetles spray a skin- and eye-irritating fluid from the abdomen.

Fig. 49 (Left). Longhorn beetles are ferocious insects with strong and sharp mandibles. The species shown here is *Batocera thomsoni*.

Fig. 50 (Left). A female *Marmessoidea rubescens* stick insect of about 10 cm in length. When disturbed, these superbly camouflaged insects defend themselves by means of a foul-smelling fluid expelled from the thorax, which causes a burning sensation on the human skin.

Fig. 51 (Right). A female *Phoebaticus serratipes*, the largest stick insect in the world, reaches an amazing 30 cm in length. The male is much smaller and winged, in contrast to the wingless female. The abilty to fly enables males to pusue potential partners.

riverine forests of the Melinau river, and is found also near Camp 5. Individual Rajah Brooke's birdwings have a territory here which includes an *Ixora* tree on which they feed. Rajah Brooke's birdwing is Sarawak's only totally protected invertebrate. It is protected because of its attraction to ruthless collectors and for the trade.

Moths are more abundant in Borneo than butterflies, with an estimated 3000 to 4000 species, of which 2400 have been recorded from Mulu (Fig. 47). Dr Jeremy Holloway of the Natural History Museum, London, is in the process of cataloguing this incredible diversity, and by the end of 2002, had published 12 special volumes dedicated to the moths of Borneo. The final number of volumes is 18. This monumental work is mainly descriptive, but also includes a wealth of information on host plants and life history.

Fig. 52 (Opposite). Lanternbugs (*Fulgora basinigra*) of the family Fulgoridae are sometimes seen in small groups on tree trunks in Mulu's lowland rain forests. The hollow, horn-like extension of the front of the head was once mistakenly believed to be luminous, hence the common name. These insects live on the sap of plants.

Beetles make up the largest order in the animal kingdom, with an amazing 350,000 described species worldwide. The named species of Coleoptera are widely considered to represent only a small fraction of the true diversity. At least 5000 species occur in Mulu.

Ground beetles (family Carabidae) can be found scavenging among the leaf litter on the forest floor in search of food, which often includes other smaller insects. Among the many forms of ground beetle, the most bizarre are probably the fiddle beetles (*Mormolyce*; subfamily Harpalinae). These have a highly flattened body and extremely elongated head, together resembling the shape of a violin (Fig. 48). Three species are found in Borneo. When attacked by predators these beetles spray a fluid with an ammonia-like smell from the abdomen which is highly irritating to the skin and eyes.

Fig. 53. Various species of caterpillars are protected against predators by poisonous hairs.

Fig. 54 (Above). The Giant forest ant (*Camponotus gigas*) can be seen on the forest floor throughout the lowland rain forest. At night, however, much greater numbers of these ants forage in the canopy overhead.

Fig. 55 (Left). Colonies of millipedes (*Pseudodesmus* sp.) feed on the fungi forming crusts on tree logs.

Longhorn beetles or longicorns are spectacular beetles because many are large, brightly coloured, and some have antennae that are as much as three times their body length. They belong to the family Cerambycidae with probably about 500 species in Borneo. *Batocera thomsoni* is a very attractive species marked with creamy yellow spots on the beige wing-case, while the thorax is decorated with two large bright red spots (Fig. 49). They are ferocious insects with strong and sharp mandibles. Among the host plants of *Batocera* are several species of wild mangoes, figs and relatives of the breadfruit tree.

Scarab beetles form a huge family, the Scarabaeidae, that contains some of the most spectacular of all Bornean insects, such as *Xylotrupes gideon*. Adults of this species have been seen to eat through palm shoots and to feed on the latex or sap that issues from wounds in the bark of trees . The caterpillar-like larvae are sometimes found in the stumps of palm trees.

Bugs are members of the order Hemiptera, another huge group of insects. They vary widely in shape, size, habits, and life history, but all have mouthparts that are adapted for piercing and sucking. The liquids they suck may be the sap of plants or the blood of animals.

Lantern bugs of the family Fulgoridae are handsome insects with often brightly coloured wings (Fig. 52). Many have the front of the head elongated to form a hollow, horn-like extension. It was once mistakenly believed that the "horn" was luminous, hence the name lantern bugs. *Pyrops intricata* is a Lantern bug that is sometimes seen in small groups on tree trunks not far above the ground in Mulu's Camp 5 area. Their staple appears to be plant sap.

Shield bugs form a large family, the Pentatomidae, and receive their name from the shape of their flattened bodies (Fig. 6). When threatened, they emit an unpleasantly smelling fluid secreted by glands on the underside of the abdomen. Many shield bugs found in Mulu are brightly coloured.

Large, almost stationary groups of up to 70 fungus-feeding millipedes (*Pseudodesmus* sp.) are found on fungus encrusted logs. Their bright yellow colouration renders the millipedes conspicuous and the reason for the formation of these groups is not evident. The millipedes may be distasteful to predators and such grouping could be for mutual defence, or alternatively digestion of the fungus could be external (i.e., on the log, after chewing by the millipedes) and might be aided by group feeding. Groups were observed to remain feeding on the same log for at least three weeks (Fig. 55). This species is confined to the riverine (alluvial) forest and virtually limited to land at or below 150 m.

Honey bees (Family Apidae) in Mulu build their nests either suspended from branches of high trees or under overhanging, high cliffs. At the Mulu Headquarters honey-combs of *Apis dorsata*, the largest honey bee in Borneo, can be seen on a *tapang* tree (*Koompassia excelsa*). This is the bees' favourite tree and the tallest tree in the world's tropical forests, with recorded heights exceeding 80 m. The main reason that the *tapang* tree is legally protected is to preserve bee nesting trees. There are also several nests under overhangs on the limestone cliffs near the bat observatory of Deer Cave. Honey from wild nests is collected and sold in markets in various parts of Borneo.

Animal life of the Mulu Caves

Cave biologists studied the organisms of the Mulu caves in relation to their very different habitats. The many habitats include clear-water stream ways, muddy canals, dry tunnels with wind-blown sand dunes and humid caverns.

Twenty-seven bat species are known from Mulu, twenty of which have their roosts in caves. The cave bats roost near cave entrances, where some light still penetrates. A well known location is in Deer Cave, where the main bat roost is betrayed by a 30-m-high pile of guano beneath a huge cavity in the ceiling of the northern chamber. Here, an enormous colony of Wrinkle-lipped bats (*Tadarida plicata*) roost during the day. Wrinkle-lipped bats have dark brown fur and a heavily wrinkled upper lip. They find their way and hunt insects by means of echolocation. Attempts to estimate their numbers are made difficult by the fact that the number of bats that fly out varies from day to day. Estimates range widely, from 600,000 to over 5 million. One of the most reliable estimates is based on photographs taken at regular intervals during the exodus and this gave 1.8 million bats.

The major caves are also home to swiftlets, mainly Mossy-nest swiftlets (*Collocalia salagana*). Edible nest swiftlets are found in small numbers only. The Mossy-nest swiftlets roost in the cave during the night and prey on insects outside during the day. Swiftlets often have their nests much deeper inside the caves than bats, in complete darkness. Around dusk the main passages are filled with the clicking sound they produce to echo-locate their way. Their commercially valueless nests are made of vegetable matter (usually mosses, liverworts, ferns etc.), cemented to the cave wall with saliva. They have a wing span of about 15 cm.

The Cave racer snake (*Elaphe taeniura*) is capable of climbing steep cave walls, and feeds on bats and swiftlets as well as on swiftlet eggs. Another bat predator is the Bat hawk (*Machaeramphus alcinus*), which performs spectacular acrobatics as it hunts bats emerging from Deer Cave at dusk. It has black plumage and an unmistakable silhouette with long, broad, pointed wings and a short, square tail.

A host of tiny creatures, including crickets, beetles, cockroaches and mites feed on the guano. Centipedes, spiders and pseudo-scorpions hunt the guano feeders. Harmless earwigs are sometimes seen on the cave floor. They really belong in the roof, where they feed on the dead skin cells of roosting bats, and sometimes fall down. In their attempts to return to the roof, they climb on any available support, including human visitors.

Deep inside the Mulu caves, where no daylight ever penetrates, live creatures without eyes. Eyeless white crabs and tiny blind beetles move about by "feeling" their way with long antennae or long legs. Bat guano is not available here, and some creatures live on organic matter brought in by percolating water, or they feed on swiftlet droppings.

PLANT LIFE

A staggering 2000 species of flowering plants, including various new species, had been identified in Mulu by 1982. From the collections made, it is estimated that the park contains at least 3500 plant species, half of which are trees and in addition more than 8000 fungi. Observations also indicate that, while the diversity is high, the distribution of any one species is often limited. This is based on a study started by Sarawak Forest Department in 1976 and continued during the 1977/1978 Sarawak Government/Royal Geographic Society expedition.

In Mulu a strong relationship is observed between vegetation types, geology—with corresponding soils—and topography. This becomes evident when the vegetation, geological and topographical maps are compared (Figs. 7, 56 & 86).

Plant life of the Gunung Mulu massif

Borneo's richest plant life is represented by the forests at the foot and on the lower slopes of Gunung Mulu (Fig. 57). These are gradually replaced, further up the mountain, by forest with reduced complexity. The change in plant life with altitude is continuous, and zonation of forest types does not correspond to specific altitudes. Below 1200 m the primary differentiation is

Fig. 56 (Opposite). Vegetation of Gunung Mulu National Park. **Fig. 57 (Following pages).** In Mulu, rivers seem as perennial as forests are vast, but this belies their common fate outside, in much of the tropics.

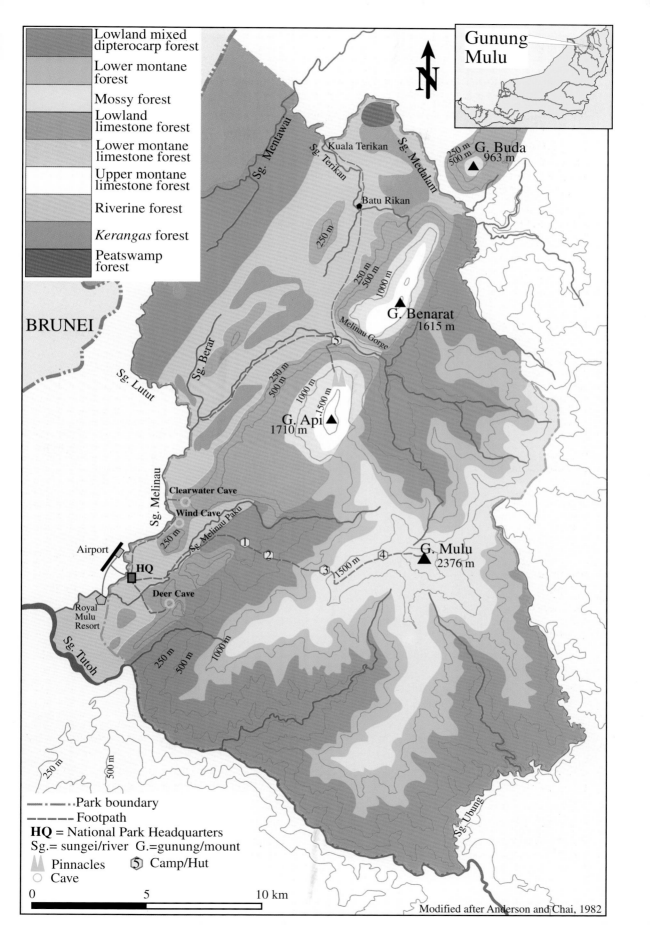

Legend:
- Lowland mixed dipterocarp forest
- Lower montane forest
- Mossy forest
- Lowland limestone forest
- Lower montane limestone forest
- Upper montane limestone forest
- Riverine forest
- *Kerangas* forest
- Peatswamp forest

Gunung Mulu

N

BRUNEI

G. Buda 963 m

G. Benarat 1615 m

G. Api 1710 m

G. Mulu 2376 m

Sg. Mentawai

Sg. Medalam

Sg. Terikan

Kuala Terikan

Batu Rikan

Melinau Gorge

Sg. Berar

Sg. Lutut

Sg. Melinau

Clearwater Cave

Wind Cave

Sg. Melinau Paku

Airport

HQ

Royal Mulu Resort

Deer Cave

Sg. Tutoh

Sg. Ubung

250 m
500 m
1000 m
1500 m

— · — Park boundary
– – – – Footpath
HQ = National Park Headquarters
Sg.= sungei/river G.=gunung/mount
Pinnacles
Cave
Camp/Hut

0   5   10 km

Modified after Anderson and Chai, 1982

Fig. 58 (Right). Huge leaves of the dipterocarp *Parashorea macrophylla*.

Fig. 59 (Below). This small tree (*Lasianthus* sp.) in Mulu's lowland rain forest is a member of the coffee family (Rubiaceae).

Fig. 60 (Opposite right). Dipterocarp fruits of the genus *Shorea* litter the forest floor.

Fig. 61 (Opposite left). A flowering parasite of the genus *Macrosolen* (Loranthaceae) adds bright colours to the pervasive green of the forest.

between ridge and slope forest. The topography of sharp ridges between branching valleys, which is typical for much of Sarawak, obscures the floral change with altitude, and influences forest height and structure. Species composition in the forest correlates most closely with soil chemistry. On protected slopes, soil development is deeper and trees tend to be larger. The canopy is usually uneven due to tall emergents. On ridges, the forest is more exposed and trees tend to be medium-sized with an even canopy. Here the transition to mountain forest begins lower than on the slopes. Soils on the shales and sandstones of the Mulu formation are dominantly sandy red-yellow podzolic soils. They are composed of varying proportions of clay and sand, with a few centimetres of decomposing plant remains on top. The yellow-orange colours are due to insoluble iron oxides.

Lowland mixed dipterocarp forest (Figs. 57–64) occurs on the lower slopes up to about 800 m where it gradually merges into lower montane forest. It can be seen, for instance, along the Mulu summit trail. On exposed ridges, the transition may occur much lower down. The upper canopy is dominated by massive trees which may reach a height of 60 m or more, and with cylindrical boles often exceeding 2.5 m girth. Most of the big trees belong to the family Dipterocarpaceae, giving this forest type its name. A very common and conspicuous dipterocarp tree on the ridges along the Mulu summit trail is *kapur bukit* (*Dryobalanops beccarii*). The yellowish-ochre to reddish bark of the massive cylindrical bole, which peels off in irregular scales of up to 60 cm long, makes it stand out among the other big trees (Fig. 64). This majestic species reaches a height of up to 55 m in Mulu (spectacular specimens of 65 m height and 6 m girth have been recorded in Brunei). It often has buttresses of several metres high. Wild relatives of the *durian,* mangosteen (or *manggis*), mango (or *asam*), rose apple (or *ubah*) and Chinese persimmon (or *kayu malam*) trees—*Durio* spp., *Garcinia* spp., *Mangifera* spp., *Syzygium* spp. and *Diospyros* spp., respectively—are particularly common. Small fan- and feather-palms (*Licuala* spp. and *Pinanga* spp., respectively) are widespread. Large woody climbers, including many rattan species, are frequently seen. Mulu's lowland rain forest is extremely rich in tree species, and 284 species (of trees exceeding 30 cm girth) were recorded in three sample plots with a combined area of only 1.2 ha.

Fig. 62 (Above).
Microporus affinis, a very common rain forest fungus.

Fig. 63 (Left). The fruiting body of a Milk-cap (*Lactarius* sp.) emerging from the moist forest floor after heavy rain. This genus is very similar to the Brittle-gills (*Russula* spp.) which exude a milky or coloured fluid when broken.

Fig. 64 (Opposite). The scaly bark of *kapur bukit* (*Dryobalanops beccarii*) is easily recognized. This is a common dipterocarp tree on the ridges along the Mulu summit trail.

Lower montane forest forms a narrow zone in the transition from the mixed dipterocarp forest to the upper montane forest. The oak and chestnut family (Fagaceae), as well as the mangosteen family (Guttiferae, with *Garcinia* fruit trees) and myrtle family (Myrtaceae, with *Syzygium* fruit trees) dominate the lower parts of this forest type. The oak, *Quercus subsericea* (Fagaceae) is here the most common large tree and its acorns are a favourite food of the Bearded pig. The palm flora includes *rattans* and wild *sago* (*Eugeissonia utilis*) which is common along the ridges. Wild *sago* is the primary source of the starch eaten by the local Penan people, who call the palm *pantu*. Ground herbs are much more common in this forest as compared to the lowland forest. The dipterocarp family is represented by only nine species in Mulu's lower montane forest sample plots. The maximum height of the canopy is about 30 m and there are few emergent trees. Tree girth is at most 180 cm, but usually less than 80 cm. However, species richness is still impressive with 226 species of trees exceeding 20 cm girth in four plots with a combined area of only 0.5 ha.

Mossy or upper montane forest is subdivided into a tall and a short type or facies, which differ in floristic composition. The tall facies of the mossy forest begins at about 1200 m on Mulu's west ridge, but on protected slopes the onset of this forest type may be significantly higher. Frequent cloud development on the mountain from this level upward soaks the forest in moisture. The soils are peaty and moist, and covered in a thick layer of moss. Mosses and lichens also cover the lower trunks of the trees and often drape the crowns (Fig. 65). The forest is dense and difficult to penetrate. The main canopy does not exceed 15 m in height and the trees are often bent or crooked. Small ferns are common. The mangosteen family (Guttiferae) and myrtle family (Myrtaceae) are particularly well represented here. Conifers, rhododendrons and herbs, particularly begonias,

Fig. 65 (Above). Mossy forest on Mulu's west ridge at about 1600 m above sea level. **Fig. 66 (Opposite).** Clusters of bird nest ferns (*Asplenium* sp.) cover the lower parts of a huge strangling fig tree.

Fig. 67. Vegetation of Mulu's summit region.

orchids, gingers, and pitcher plants are characteristic of the mossy forest (Fig. 90). Species richness shows a marked decrease compared to the lower montane forest, with 155 species of trees (over 10 cm girth) recorded in five plots with a combined area of 0.4 ha.

The short facies of the mossy forest is found on exposed ridges upward from about 1600 m and on sheltered slopes upward from about 1900 m. The height of the trees no longer exceeds 9 m. Here, the mossy forest is even denser. Near the ground there is often a layer of moss-covered tree trunks which grow sub-horizontally and have sucker shoots which produce new trees. Here also are tree ferns. Species composition within the short mossy forest varies with both altitude and exposure. The oak family (Fagaceae) and myrtle family (Myrtaceae) together with the conifer family (Podocarpaceae) initially dominate the tree flora. Further up, the last two of these families together with the heather family (Ericaceae) and mangosteen family (Guttiferae) are abundant.

Summit zone vegetation (Fig. 67) is found above about 2200 m altitude and consists of shrubs, at most three metres in height, dominated by rhododendrons (Ericaceae). There are a few stunted trees attaining a height of 5 m, including a conifer. Ten species of pitcher plant are found in Mulu, including *Nepenthes muluensis* which only occurs in the summit region and was first described as recently as 1966. The only other locations where *N. muluensis* has been collected are Gunung

Murud (Sarawak's highest mountain) and Bukit Batu Lawi. In the dense vegetation of the summit region, exquisite orchids grow near the ground, sheltered from the wind by the hardy shrubs. A total of 26 species of trees and shrubs have been recorded in the summit zone.

Plant life of the Melinau limestone

The plant life of the Melinau limestone is distinctive and contains many species restricted to the park. These plants have evolved in an isolated environment as the limestone on which they live is like an island in a sea of shales and sandstones that dominate the subsurface in most of Sarawak. Soils on the Melinau limestone are usually thin and discontinuous, and consist mainly of silt or clay loams (a somewhat plastic mixture of clay, silt, and sand), with or without limestone fragments. Organic matter content of the soil generally increases with altitude. There are five different habitats, the three most accessible of which are outlined below.

Lowland limestone forest occurs on the slopes of the limestone massifs up to about 800 m altitude (Fig. 69). It can be seen, for instance, along the trail to the Pinnacles of Gunung Api, above Camp 5. On moderate slopes (less than 45°) the forest is dominated by large, emergent trees that may attain a height of 40 m and exceed 2.5 m in girth. The dipterocarp family dominates, and includes species with a limestone affinity such as *Hopea andersonii*, but also species commonly found in

Fig. 68. In Gunung Mulu's summit region, the pitcher plant *Nepenthes muluensis* drapes all over bushy rhododendron in exposed sites. **Fig. 69 (Following pages).** Typical forest of the broken terrain on the lower slopes of Mulu's limestone mountains.

Fig. 70 (Right). Single-leafed plants of the genus *Monophyllea* are common along many of the trails traversing limestone.

Fig. 71 (Left). A beautiful *Begonia conipilia* with its attractive, velvety hairy leaves and delicate flowers grows in the semi-shady limestone rockface.

mixed dipterocarp forest such as *Shorea multiflora*. Typical limestone species in the Tiliaceae and Sapotaceae families are also important. Large woody climbers are less common than in mixed dipterocarp forest and rattans are very rare. There is little undergrowth, and the leaf litter forms a thick layer. One-leafed plants of the genus *Monophyllaea* grow on exposed rocks. These are rare herbs which have specialised tissue for the preservation of water and they are only found in limestone forest (Fig. 70). *Amorphophallus cf. lambii* is an aroid (Family Araceae) found in Mulu's limestone forest (Fig. 73). When the single leaf dies, the plant produces a spectacular inflorescence, standing on a stalk about 1.5 m above the forest floor. The inflorescence is slightly malodorous, which attracts small beetles that are its pollinators. On very steep slopes (exceeding 45°) lowland limestone forest becomes thick and dense and consists of many small trees with abundant shrubs. On low, near-vertical cliffs that are protected from exposure by surrounding tall trees, the cliff walls are often draped in a cover of herbs. This is the habitat of an extraordinary limestone-specific orchid, *Paphiopedilum sanderianum*, with long, dangling petals that can reach a metre or more in length (Fig. 72). Its strict habitat requirements may explain its rarity.

Lower montane limestone forest occurs from about 800 m elevation up to about 1200 m, but there are no sharp boundaries. The rocks tend to be more exposed than lower down, revealing large limestone blocks and small ravines. As on Gunung Mulu, the height of the tree crowns and the average size of the trees decrease gradually with increasing elevation. The forest is dense and composed of small trees with a canopy height of less than 25 m. Tree girth rarely exceeds 1.5 m.

Fig. 72 (Right). One of the most striking of all orchids, *Paphiopedilum sanderianum* has long, dangling petals that can reach a metre or more in length. This species grows only on limestone cliffs and only in places that are in deep shade for most of the day. These strict habitat requirements may explain its rarity. Sadly, unscrupulous orchid collectors have taken numerous plants from many accessible sites.

Fig. 73 (Left). This extraordinary plant, *Amorphophallus cf. lambii*, is often seen in Mulu's limestone forest. When the single leaf dies the plant produces a spectacular inflorescence on a stalk at breast height above the forest floor. Subsequently the berry-like fruits seen in the photograph appear.

Trees are often bent and twisted. Only one species, *Hopea argentea*, of the dipterocarp family has been recorded here. The plant life is mainly composed of non-limestone species. For example, *upi paya* (*Parishia maingayi*) of the mango family (Anacardiaceae) is abundant. It has characteristic brown, hairy fruits with long wings. An easily recognised tree in this forest is *selunsor padang* (*Tristaniopsis obovata*), with orange-brown smooth bark. The bark peels off in long scroll-like pieces and accumulates around the base of the trunk. The leaf litter layer is thick. Shrubs and herbs are abundant. Orchids and ferns drape the lower trunks of many trees.

Upper montane limestone forest occurs upward from roughly 1200 m altitude. The terrain is here exceedingly broken and there is much exposed rock. The Pinnacles of Gunung Api form part of this terrain (Fig. 74). The forest here is the limestone equivalent of the mossy forest on Gunung Mulu. In places where a deep humus layer has developed, it is covered in mosses that also drape the small trees and shrubs. No consistent canopy develops due to the broken terrain. There are several facies of different tree height and floristic composition. Non limestone-specific species dominate, and the principal species are mostly the same as those found on Gunung Mulu at equivalent heights. However, three species of Screw-pine (*Pandanus* spp., Pandanaceae) are abundant here. Extensive stands of almost pure *Pandanus* may have resulted from fires that destroyed the former vegetation. Several of Mulu's ten species of pitcher plants can be seen at the side of the trail that leads to the pinnacles. The large pitcher plant *Nepenthes stenophylla,* which is confined to Borneo, is conspicuous in more open localities. It clambers on rocks, shrubs and into the small trees. On the flat plateau beneath the summit of Gunung Api (at about 1520 m altitude), the vegetation consists of a low carpet, at most one metre in height, of shrubs (including three species of *Rhododendron*), orchids and screw-pines.

Plant life of the alluvial (or riverine) plain

There are three major forest types on the alluvial plain in the valley of the Melinau river. Distribution of these forest types is strongly influenced by soil development. Lowland riverine forest occurs on frequently flooded, recent river sediments. Here soils vary greatly but essentially consist of clay with various percentages of silt and sand. Most of these soils are at least partly waterlogged with a resulting grey colour. *Kerangas* forest is found on raised, flat-lying terraces. Several phases of uplift during the last two million years have caused the rivers to cut into their own sediments, leaving behind these terraces. On the terraces, soils are mainly sandy with various proportions of clay, silt and humus. Drainage varies from poor to good. Peatswamp forest occurs where drainage is impeded and shallow peat (up to 1.2 m in depth) has formed.

Lowland riverine forest is common in the floodplain of the Melinau river (Fig. 79). It can be seen, for instance, along the trail to

Fig. 74 (Above). In the pinnacles terrain, the soil consists of thin pockets of humus or shallow brown clay on bare, hard rock.

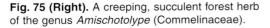

Fig. 75 (Right). A creeping, succulent forest herb of the genus *Amischotolype* (Commelinaceae).

Fig. 76. Ironwood or *belian* tree (*Eusideroxylon malagangai*), one of the largest trees in the riverine forest.
Fig. 77 (inset). Fruiting trees are easily recognized by the distinctive shape of the fruits.

Fig. 78. Remnants of *Shorea* flowers on the forest floor.

Camp 5 (see the route description to the Pinnacles of Gunung Api) where it partly consists of old secondary forest. This forest type mirrors a great variation in soils, and is probably the most complex forest type in the park. On the grey soils, which are the most widespread soils in the floodplain, the forest has a rather open, uneven canopy with emerging trees up to 40 m in height, and up to 2.5 m in girth. Many large trees are heavily buttressed and some trees have stilt roots. A characteristic non-buttressed species is *Eusideroxylon malagangai* (Lauraceae), one of the two Bornean ironwood or *belian* species, and this is one of the largest trees in this forest (Figs. 76 & 77). A common large dipterocarp tree is the *peran* (*Parashorea macrophylla*), recognisable from its pleated leaves which are up to 35 cm long (Fig. 58).

Mulu's riverine forest contains an abundance of fig trees (*Ficus* sp.). Some of these, the strangling figs, are found throughout the forest and can easily be recognised from their often spectacular lattice-like trunks and large size (Figs. 22, 80 & 83). "Stem figs" are less widely distributed and are mainly found along streams and along the fringes of the forest. When fruiting, these can be distinguished by the bunches of figs borne on the trunk or major branches (Figs. 81 & 82). The well-disguised "earth figs" bear fruit on runners which are usually partly embedded in the soil. These are also found along streams and on rocky cliffs and landslips at the fringe of the forest. Ecologically the figs play a key role in the forest by providing sufficient food for many animals, in particular birds and mammals, during periods of scarcity of other fruits. Strangling figs usually begin life on other trees and eventually may strangle them to death. Most of the so-called strangling figs, however, do not encircle and kill the host tree. The more common species only send down a pillar root near the host trunk.

Large woody climbers, rattans and epiphytes are common. Due to the often rather open canopy, enough light reaches the forest floor to allow luxuriant undergrowth, including small palms and gingers. In densely shaded places the undergrowth is less thick and here some spectacular orchids can be found.

Fig. 79 (Opposite top). Riverine forest by a small tributary of the Melinau Paku river. **Fig. 80 (Lower right).** Roots of a strangling fig in the early stage of developing a lattice structure around the trunk of the host tree (*Alstonia* sp.). **Fig. 81 (Lower left).** Bunches of figs borne on the trunk of a stem fig in riverine forest. **Fig. 82 (inset).** Ants exploit the food resources associated with ripe figs, which include fig wasps.

Kerangas or tropical heath forest occurs on terraces raised above the present floodplain of the rivers. This forest type is highly variable in appearance, depending on soil properties and drainage conditions. It is mainly composed of medium-sized and small trees, with a generally even canopy and few emergents. The much smaller size of trees compared to mixed dipterocarp forest often gives a pole-like appearance, giving the impression of a dense tree plantation. Young trees, palms (including rattans), pandans, pitcher plants, and shrubs form a moderately dense understorey. Some rattans are *kerangas*-specific. The dipterocarp *alan* (*Shorea albida*) is the principal dominant and the most characteristic tree species. It has purplish to greyish, deeply fissured bark. It may develop into a very large emergent tree—up to 2.5 m in girth—with tall buttresses spreading as large surface roots. Two species of *bintangor* (*Calophyllum* spp., Guttiferae) also reach canopy height. These can be recognised from the leathery, shiny leaves, in which the veins are close together and run parallel. The fruits of two tall *rengas* trees (*Gluta* spp., Anacardiaceae) can be recognised from their reddish wings. The genus *Gluta*—*gluten* is Latin for 'glue'—derives its name from the irritant, sticky exudate which, when exposed to the air, often forms lacquer-like droplets or black stains on the bark.

Peatswamp forest is found in a small area between the Tarikan and Medalam rivers. It has many of the characteristics of the vast peatswamp forests typical of Sarawak's river deltas. A special feature of these peatswamp forests (including those in Mulu) is a concentric zonation of four or more forest types, which is attributed to decreasing fertility of the peat soils towards the centre. Structure and floristic composition of the forest change from the outer rim to the centre of the swamp and there is also a decrease in the size of all trees.

The outer rim has mixed swamp forest with an uneven canopy of about 32 m height. Among the principal dominant trees are large dipterocarps such as *kapur paya* (*Dryobalanops rappa*), *alan* (*Shorea albida*) and *meranti paya* (*Shorea platycarpa*), and trees in the genera *Gluta* and *Calophyllum*. This is succeeded by increasingly dense forest with an even, but broken canopy of about 28 m high. It has several canopy species in common with the outer rim. *Pandanus andersonii*, recognisable by its long, slender leaves and stilt-like roots, is widespread and forms dense thickets in the lower story. The leaf litter covers a "platform" of roots which is raised above the true swamp surface. Further towards the centre of the swamp is a forest composed of numerous small trees of fewer species, with an uneven canopy of about 20 m height. The species are common to those of the previously described forest, but pandans are sparse. In the centre of the swamp is a zone of small, stunted trees, usually not more than 10 m in height. The few larger trees are invariably *keruntum* (*Combretocarpus rotundatus*), an inland mangrove species of the Anisophylleaceae family. Peat is exposed in places and pandans occur scattered through this forest.

Plant life of the Setap shales

In the northwestern part of the park, bordering on Brunei, there are extensive areas of the Setap shale formation, partly overlain by dissected, raised terraces of river sediments. The soils on the Setap shale are comparable to those at low elevations on Gunung Mulu while those on the high terraces are similar to those on the terraces in the alluvial plain. On the Setap shale occurs mixed dipterocarp forest of similar structure but different floristic composition compared to the lowland mixed dipterocarp forest on Gunung Mulu, although the two have many species in common. On the high terraces occurs *kerangas* forest with structure, density and floristic composition akin to the *kerangas* forest found on the low terraces in the alluvial plain.

Fig. 83 (Opposite). The enormous trunk of a strangling fig lends support to a host of other plants.

Climate and Rocks

CLIMATE

Sarawak

The equator crosses Borneo less than one degree south of Sarawak, and the whole island has an equatorial climate. Temperatures are uniformly high at sea level, with daily variations between around 22°C just before dawn to around 32°C in the early afternoon. Thus, in the open, the daily range is about 10°C. Under high forest, however, the ground is protected from direct sunlight and the afternoons are cooler. Here, the daily range is much smaller, about 2°C to 3°C at ground level.

Although Sarawak does not normally experience a distinct dry season, two relatively wetter (monsoon) seasons and two intervening, relatively dryer seasons do occur. The arrival and duration of the individual seasons varies very much from year to year, so the months given are approximate. The northeast monsoon (November to February/March) brings the heaviest rainfall of the year with winds blowing typically from the northeast. During the relatively dryer transition (April and May), the winds are light (except during occasional squalls) and variable in direction. The southwest monsoon (June to September), with predominantly southwest winds, is normally quieter than the northeast monsoon, but also gives occasional surges and periods of unsettled weather. During the relatively drier transition (October and November), the wind direction is changeable with an increase in wind speed and frequency of squalls.

Mulu

Due to Mulu's inland location, at about 100 km from the coast, and due to the influence of its mountains, Mulu's climate is wetter than that of most other parts of Sarawak. Meteorological observations were made at various locations and altitudes within the park during one year (August 1977–August 1978) as part of the Sarawak Government/Royal Geographic Society expedition. Annual rainfall in the park in 1977–1978 was very high (4482 to 6802 mm) and considerably higher than in the surrounding lowland areas of Sarawak. Rainfall appears to increase with altitude up to about 1700 m, but then decreases at higher altitude. Short dry periods were noted during the relatively less rainy season of the southwest monsoon (August/September). These may be of considerable ecological significance because water deficits may develop in the shallow soils of the steep slopes. Regular periods of water stress may have a controlling influence on the type of vegetation that can exist in such locations.

GEOLOGY

As shown on the geological map, Mulu's subsurface consists of several different rock types (Fig. 86). Each rock type has distinctive properties which ultimately result in the dramatic differences seen in Mulu's landscapes, soils and vegetation types (Fig. 88).

A variety of rock types

The Gunung Mulu massif occupies the entire southeastern half of the park. This is made up of shales (claystones which split into thin layers) and interbedded sandstones. Together these

---

Fig. 84 (Opposite). South face of Gunung Benarat as seen from the Melinau Gorge.

77

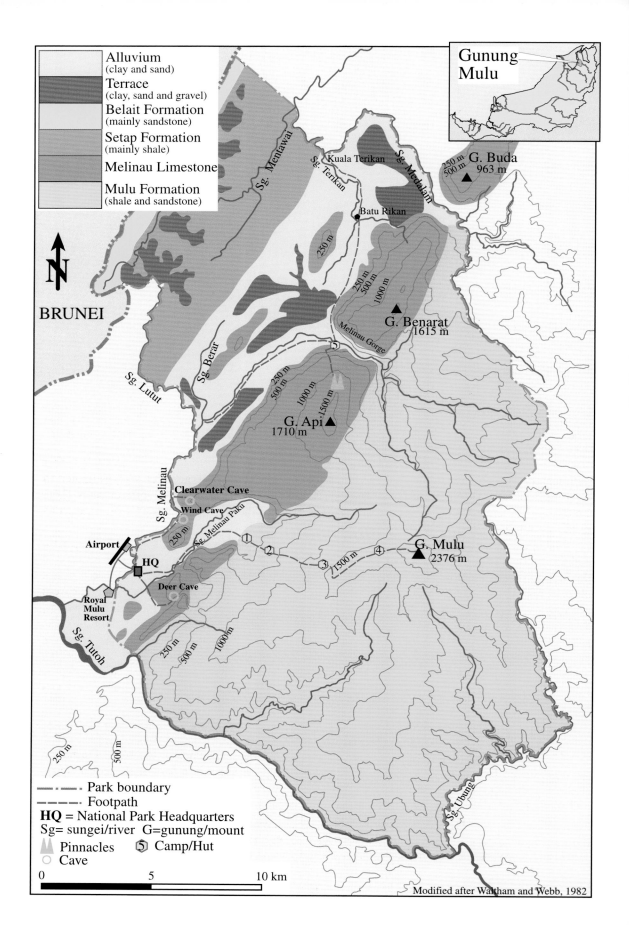

Gunung Mulu

Alluvium (clay and sand)
Terrace (clay, sand and gravel)
Belait Formation (mainly sandstone)
Setap Formation (mainly shale)
Melinau Limestone
Mulu Formation (shale and sandstone)

N

BRUNEI

Sg. Meniawai
Sg. Terikan
Kuala Terikan
Sg. Medalam
250 m
500 m
G. Buda
963 m
Batu Rikan
250 m
250 m
500 m
1000 m
G. Benarat
1615 m
Sg. Berar
Melinau Gorge
Sg. Lutut
250 m
500 m
1000 m
1500 m
G. Api
1710 m
Sg. Melinau
Clearwater Cave
Wind Cave
Sg. Melinau Paku
1
2
3
4
G. Mulu
2376 m
1500 m
Airport
HQ
250 m
Deer Cave
Royal Mulu Resort
Sg. Tutoh
250 m
500 m
1000 m
250 m
500 m
1000 m
250 m
500 m
Sg. Ubung

—··—··— Park boundary
— — — Footpath
HQ = National Park Headquarters
Sg= sungei/river G=gunung/mount
Pinnacles
Camp/Hut
Cave

0   5   10 km

Modified after Waltham and Webb, 1982

Fig. 85. Gunung Benarat's precipitous limestone cliffs line the Melinau Gorge. The Melinau river can be seen to flow from the gorge, where it is a turbulent white-water river, into a flat flood plain, where it becomes a gently-flowing, meandering stream.

sedimentary rocks comprise the Mulu Formation, which has an enormous thickness, estimated to be some 4000 to 5000 m. Microfossils indicate an age of between 40 and 90 million years (Late Cretaceous to Late Eocene). Sandy soils have developed on the Mulu Formation rocks. The flanks of the mountain are dissected with steep valleys that form branching patterns.

The spectacular line of mountains comprising Gunung Buda, Gunung Benarat, Gunung Api, and the southern limestone hills is made up of the Melinau Limestone Formation. Gunung Api is the highest limestone mountain at 1710 m. These mountains are in places bounded by precipitous cliffs as high as 600 m (Figs. 84 & 85). The limestone landscapes are extremely rugged, and here are some of the world's finest examples of limestone weathering. Forty-five-metre-tall pinnacles, giant caves, deep gorges, overhanging cliffs, and deep vertical shafts are some of the highlights (Fig. 87). Peaty soils have developed in patches. Most drainage is underground. In the northwestern part of the park, overlying the Melinau limestone, there are dark grey or blackish shales with minor sandstones of the Setap Shale Formation. Outside the park, the Setap shale is fully exposed, and its thickness is estimated at 4000 to 5000 m. The landscape formed by the Setap shale is marked by small sandstone ridges alternating with broad valleys.

Seas, lagoons and coral reefs

The clay and sand that ultimately formed the shales and sandstones of the Mulu Formation were deposited for the most part in a deep sea, although in the upper part of the Formation a shallow marine origin is probable. By about 40 million years ago (Late Eocene), the influx of clay and sand ceased in the Mulu area and the sea water became clear enough and the sea bed shallow

Fig. 86 (Opposite). Geology of Gunung Mulu National Park. **Fig. 87 (Following pages).** This sinkhole is one of the many limestone weathering features that honeycomb Mulu's limestone mountains.

enough for corals to grow and seashells to accumulate. The build-up of the reef continued for a very long time, estimated at about 20 million years, indicating persisting geological stability of the region. The Melinau Limestone was formed where coral reefs and, behind these, quiet lagoons exised. It is a huge lens-shaped body with a maximum thickness of about 1500 m. It consists mainly of fine calcite particles, but in places fossil corals, shells (foraminifera, bivalves and gastropods), and algal balls are abundant. Fossils can best be seen in the caves, as on the surface they are obscured by a white patina due to weathering. Micro-fossils indicate an age of between 17 and 40 million years (Late Eocene to Early Miocene).

Uplift, folding and erosion

The main uplift and folding in the Mulu region took place from 10 to 2 million years ago (Late Miocene and Pliocene). The dominant folds in all the rock formations trend parallel to the line of limestone mountains (northeast-southwest). As a result of the uplift, an enormous thickness of Setap shale, Melinau limestone, and other formations (exposed outside the park) was

Fig. 88. The sharp-edged silhouette of the Gunung Mulu sandstone massif towers over the more rounded limestone mountains which contain Mulu's caves.

eroded off the Gunung Mulu massif. The high pressure and temperature during long periods of deep burial (before uplift took place) caused the clay in the Mulu Formation to change its properties and become shale. Among other things it became much harder and developed a strong tendency to split.

Uplift of mountains causes rivers to cut their channels deeper. Conversely, when the uplift declines, rivers fill-in their channels and valleys. Following the main uplift and erosion in the Mulu region, extensive sediments were laid down by the Melinau river, its tributaries and other rivers, resulting in a large alluvial fan. Build-up of this fan happened in periods of high rainfall that can be correlated to intervals between the ice ages of Europe and North America. During the ice ages, the climate in Borneo was relatively dry and the rivers cut into their own sediments, leaving terraces tens of metres above the present river levels. These terraces consist mainly of gravel and of sandstone cobbles embedded in sand and clay. On the terraces, soils are sandy and well drained. Floodplains exist in the lowest parts of the valleys. During the rainy season, these are often inundated, and more clay and silt is deposited as alluvium.

Origin of the Pinnacles

The rock surfaces of the limestone mountains lack soil cover over considerable areas. Hardy trees are rooted in crevices and small patches of organic soil. The limestone is dissected by deep

Fig. 89 (Opposite). *Rhododendron cf. orbiculatum* grows in exposed locations on Mulu's west ridge.

vertical fissures which are gradually enlarged. In areas where the limestone is particularly homogeneous and massive, and the vertical fractures are widely spaced, heavy rainfall deepens the fractures into V-shaped crevices. Large, strong and intact blocks of limestone are thus isolated. As the overall rock surface is slowly lowered, the steep sides of the crevices eventually intersect at the crest of the block. This gives the characteristic form of the pinnacles. They are best developed at about 1200 m altitude on the northern end of Gunung Api, where they reach exceptional sizes of 45 m in height and 20 m in width at the base. Their shapes are here sharply pointed or bladed. Their upper surfaces are grooved and the lower surfaces, below the vegetation line, are intensely pitted in a honeycomb-like surface. They cannot be climbed without special aids and the Pinnacles terrain is virtually impenetrable. Pinnacles of various sizes are developed over much of the higher slopes of Gunung Api and Gunung Benarat.

Origin of the Mulu Caves

All caves in the limestone massifs of Gunung Benarat, Gunung Api and the southern hills were formed by running water. Rain water percolates through faults and joints and along bedding planes (surfaces of original deposition of the limestone). Rainwater is slightly acidic and as it trickles through these fractures and along bedding planes, it dissolves calcium carbonate, (a process helped by the high tropical temperatures). The water of streams and rivers finds its way through channels thus formed and erodes these into larger underground passages. The continuously eroding force of water flowing through limestone is illustrated by the Clearwater river which, in low flow, carries about 27 kg of dissolved limestone out of the cave per minute. As the limestone is virtually free of silt, the river remains transparent.

Like their surface counterparts, underground rivers cut their channels deeper driven by uplift of the mountains. This eventually resulted in Mulu's huge stream passages. Partly eroded gravel beds inside the caves are relics of periods of high rainfall when a large alluvial fan was built-up.

Grooves high up the walls of some caves, e.g., in Clearwater cave, were etched by the underground river when it flowed at much higher levels long ago. Where the cave bends sharply, the grooves appear as deep notches on the cave walls. These marks of high river levels correspond to phases of build-up of the alluvial fan.

Estimating the age of the caves

An estimate of the age of the caves can be derived from an examination of the gravel beds found in underground passages. The passages were formed by the river long ago but have subsequently been abandoned. Such passages are known as fossil underground passages. In places, they can be seen at heights of 400 m above the level at which the river now appears at the surface. For example, the entrance to the Tiger Cave passage can be seen on the Benarat cliff in the Melinau Gorge high above the present Melinau river.

During the 1991 Mulu Caves expedition, clay samples were taken from gravel beds in the highest fossil passages. Iron-rich clay particles are slightly magnetic, and when they settle from muddy, stagnant water, they orientate themselves like small compass needles. The earth's magnetic field has reversed itself many times in geological history. This well-documented pattern of reversals can be used for estimating the age of sediments. The result, however, gives an age for deposition of the clay, and the cave passage itself therefore may be significantly older. Results show, that underground rivers have cut into the Mulu limestone over a period of at least 2 million years. This gives a rate of about 1 cm in 50 years at which the underground rivers have lowered their drainage.

Why are Mulu's caves so big?

The world's largest underground chamber, the Sarawak Chamber, is 400 m wide and 600 m long. The ceiling and floor are sloping, and the height measured from the lowest part of the floor to the highest part of the ceiling is about 270 m. Many other caves in Mulu are also huge by world standards. The slopes of the Gunung Mulu sandstone massif to the east provide a steeply graded drainage pattern that goes directly through the limestone massifs. The combination of a tropical climate with very high rainfall (up to 6800 mm/year) and the steeply graded drainage provides an optimum environment for cave development. The Melinau limestone itself is very hard and massive, and so the roof of a cave does not easily collapse. The limestone also has relatively few widely spaced fractures, which develop into fewer and larger caves rather than would many closely spaced fractures. The combination of the above factors has resulted in Mulu's world-class caves.

Fig. 90. Delicate flowers of *Bulbophyllum* aff. *farinulentum*, an orchid growing as an epiphyte in mossy forest on Mulu's west ridge.

Prehistory

Brief archaeological surveys in 1977/1978 by the Sarawak Museum revealed that some of the Mulu caves (including Deer Cave) were used as burial sites in relatively recent times. Finds from the floor of some caves were mainly imported Chinese ceramics. The first systematic archaeological excavations in Mulu were done in 1989, in the Cave of Winds. The excavations show that the cave was used for burials between 3000 and 1500 years ago. Burial items found include three-colour pieces of pottery, double-spouted vessels, iron artifacts (probably fragments of knives), coloured glass beads and sea shells (bivalves). From the finds, it is inferred that the people who buried their dead here probably practised agriculture, but also collected wild food plants and hunted animals.

Fig. 91. Visitor facilities at Mulu culminate in the Royal Mulu Resort.

Acknowledgements

Foremost we would like to thank Mr. Cheong Ek Choon, Director, Sarawak Forest Department, and his staff, who provided multitudinous help in the national park as well as in the office. Mr. Sapuan Hj. Ahmad, formerly Head of the National Parks and Wildlife Division, has greatly supported and encouraged the book project. Mr. Suliman Hj. Jamahari, Park Warden, and Mr. Sem Pasan, Deputy Park Warden, provided valuable advice during the work in 2002. Mr. Brian Clark, Manager and Mr. Greg Martindale, Conservation Manager, Gunung Mulu National Park, commented on the manuscript and gave useful suggestions. We thank Dr. Elizabeth Bennett, WCI/Sarawak Forest Department, who edited the fauna section; Dr. Paul Chai, International Tropical Timber Organization, who edited the section on Mulu's plant life; Datuk C.L. Chan, the publisher, who contributed significantly to the technical contents of the book and identified the stick insects and lantern bug. Dr. Arthur Chung and Mr. Richard Ansis of the Forest Research Centre, Sepilok, identified the moth. Dr. Lee Su See of FRIM named the fungi and Dr. Jaap Vermuelen of the Singapore Botanic Garden determined the *Bulbophyllum* orchid. Mr. David W. Gill, formerly with the Sarawak Forest Department, who edited the section on the caves of Mulu; Mr. Abang Hamid, formerly Assistant Director, Sarawak Forest Research Centre, who edited the section on insects; Dr. K.M. Wong of the Rimba Ilmu Botanic Garden, Institute of Biological Sciences, University of Malaya, Kuala Lumpur, very kindly edited the entire manuscript; Mr. Tony Sebastian and Mr. Daniel Kong, who identified birds from the slides. Thanks are also due to Mr. Paulus Banda Ngau, Mr. William Bangit, Mr. Jau Bilong, Mr. Joseph Lagang, Mr. Laing Lawai, Mr. Sayan Lucin, Mr. Michael Malang, and Mr. David Steven Wan Emang for their help on Batu Bungan, Gunung Mulu and Gunung Api. We are grateful to the management of the Royal Mulu Resort who kindly provided accommodation during the work in the park in 2002.

Useful Addresses

Visitors' Information Centre. Jalan Masjid, Kuching. Tel: 6082-248088
Visitors' Information Centre. Lot 452, Jalan Melayu, Miri. Tel: 6085-434184/434180

Further Reading

Hazebroek, H.P. and Kashim, A.A.M. (2000). *National Parks of Sarawak.* Natural History Publications (Borneo), Kota Kinabalu. xii + 502 pp.

Inger, R.F. and Stuebing, R.B. (1997). *A Field Guide to the Frogs of Borneo.* Natural History Publications (Borneo), Kota Kinabalu. x + 207 pp.

Inger, R.F. and Tan, F.L. (1996). *The Natural History of Amphibians and Reptiles in Sabah.* Natural History Publications (Borneo), Kota Kinabalu. iv + 101 pp.

MacKinnon, J. and Phillipps, K. (1993). *A Field Guide to the Birds of Borneo, Sumatra, Java and Bali.* Oxford University Press, Oxford. 491 pp.

Payne, J., Francis, C.M. and Phillipps, K. (1985). *A Field Guide to the Mammals of Borneo.* The Sabah Society, Kota Kinabalu and Worldwide Fund for Nature Malaysia, Kuala Lumpur. 332 pp.

Smythies, B.E. (1999). *The Birds of Borneo.* 4th Edition. Natural History Publications (Borneo), in association with the Sabah Society, Kota Kinabalu. xii + 473 pp.

Stuebing, R.B. and Inger, R.F. (1999). *A Field Guide to the Snakes of Borneo.* Natural History Publications (Borneo), Kota Kinabalu. viii + 254 pp.

Checklist of Mammals

(Based on: Anderson, J.A.R., Jermy, A.C. & Cranbrook, Earl of (1982) Gunung Mulu National Park—A Management and Development Plan. Royal Geographic Society, London. 327 pp.)

INSECTIVORES

Moonrat (*Echinosorex gymnurus*)
Lesser Gymnure (*Hylomys auillus*)
Savi's Pigmy Shrew (*Suncus etruscus*)
Sunda Shrew (*Crocidura monticola*)
Mountain Treeshrew (*Tupaia Montana*)
Painted Treeshrew (*T. picta*)
Smooth-tailed Treeshrew (*Dendrogale melanura*)

COLUGOS

Flying Lemur (*Cynocephalus variegates*)

BATS

Flying Fox (*Pteropus vampyrua*)
Malaysian Fruit Bat (*Cyanopterus brachyotis*)
Spotted-winged Fruit Bat (*Balionycteris maculata*)
Grey Fruit Bat (*Aethalops alecto*)
Dusky Fruit Bat (*Penthetor lucasii*)
Borneo Horseshoe Bat (*Rhinolophus borneensis*)
Creagh's Horseshoe Bat (*R. creaghi*)
Philippine Horseshoe Bat (*R. philippensis*)
Lesser Tailless Horseshoe Bat (*Coelops robinsoni*)
Cantor's Roundleaf Horseshoe Bat (*Hipposideros galeritus*)
Lyon's Round]eaf Horseshoe Bat (*H. insolens*)
Diadem Roundleaf Horseshoe Bat (*H. diadema*)
Horsfield's Bat (*Myotis horsfieldii*)
Short-winged Brown Bat (*Philetor brachypterus*)
Round-eared Tube-nosed Bat (*Murina cyclotis*)
Wrinkled-lipped Bat (*Tadarida plicata*)

MONKEYS, APES & RELATIVES

Western Tarsier (*Tarsius bancanus*)
Grey Leaf Monkey (*Presbytis hosei*)
Maroon Leaf Monkey (*P. rubicunda*)
Silvered Leaf Monkey (*P. cristata*)
Long-tailed Macaque (*Macaca fascicularis*)
Pig-tailed Macaque (*M. nemestrina*)
Bornean Gibbon (*Hylobates muelleri*)
Slow Loris (*Nycticebus coucang*)

RODENTS

Giant Squirrel (*Ratufa affinis*)
Prevost's Squirrel (*Callosciurus prevostii*)
Kinabalu Squirrel (*C. baluensis*)
Plantain Squirrel (*C. notatus*)
Horse-tailed Squirrel (*Sundasciurus hippurus*)
Jentink's Squirrel (*S. jentinki*)
Three-striped Ground Squirrel (*Lariscus insignis*)
Bornean Mountain Ground Squirrel (*Dremomys everetti*)
Plain Pigmy Squirrel (*Exilisciurus exilis*)
Whitehead's Pigmy Squirrel (*E. whiteheadi*)
Tufted Ground Squirrel (*Rheithrosciurus macrotis*)
Black Giant Flying Squirrel (*Aeromys tephromelas*)
Müller's Rat (*Rattus muelleri*)
Mountain Giant Rat (*R. infraluteus*)
Dark-tailed Tree Rat (*R. cremoriventer*)
Red Spiny Rat (*R. surifer*)
Whitehead's Rat (*R. whiteheadi*)
Mountain Long-tailed Rat (*R. rapit*)
Long-tailed Giant Rat (*R. sabanus*)
Tree-mouse (unidentified) (*Chiropocomys gliroides*)
Long-tailed Porcupine (*Trichys lipura*)
Large porcupines (not positively identified) (*Hysterix/Thecurus*)

CARNIVORES

Sun Bear (*Helarctos malayanus*)
Yellow-throated Marten (*Martes flaviqula*)
Otters (not positively identified) (*Lutra* sp./*Amblonyx*)
Malay Civet (*Viverra tangalunga*)
Common Palm Civet (*Paradoxurus hermaphroditus*)
Bearcat (*Arctictis binturong*)
Three-striped Palm Civet (*Arctogalidia trivirgata*)
Banded Palm Civet (*Hemigalus derbyanus*)
Mongoose (*Herpestes* sp.)

CLOVEN-HOOFED UNGULATES

Bearded Pig (*Sus barbatus*)
(Lesser) Mouse-deer (*Tragulus* sp. cf. *javanicus*)
Barking Deer (*Muntiacus muntjak*)
Sambar Deer (*Cervus unicolor*)

Checklist of Birds

(Based on: Anderson, J.A.R., Jermy, A.C. & Cranbrook, Earl of (1982) Gunung Mulu National Park—A Management and Development Plan. Royal Geographic Society, London. 327 pp.)

CORMORANTS & ALLIES (Pelecaniformes)
Darter (*Anhinga melanogaster*)

HERONS & STORKS (Ardeiformes)
Little Green Heron (*Butorides striatus*)
Tiger Bittern (*Goisakiua melanolophus*)
Storm's Stork (*Ciconia stormi*)

HAWKS & EAGLES (Falconiformes)
Bat Hawk (*Macheiramphus alcinus*)
Honey Buzzard (*Pernis ptilorhyncus*)
Brahminy Kite (*Haliastur Indus*)
Crested Goshawk (*Accipiter trivirgatus*)
Asiatic Sparrowhawk (*A. virgatus*)
Blyth's Hawk Eagle (*Spizeetus alboniger*)
(Wallace's) Hawk Eagle (*S. cf. nanus*)
Black Eagle (*Ictinaetus malayensis*)
Lesser Fish Eagle (*Icthyophaga humilis*)
Crested Serpent Eagle (*Spilornia cheela*)
Kinabalu Serpent Eagle (*S. kinabaluensis*)
Black-thighed (Common) Falconet (*Microhierax fringillarius*)
Peregrine Falcon (*Falco peregrinus*)

PHEASANTS & PARTRIDGES (Galliformes)
Red-breasted Tree Partridge (*Arborophila hyperythra*)
Black Wood Partridge (*Melanoperdix nigra*)
Crested Green Wood Partridge (*Rollulus rouloul*)
Crimson-headed Wood Partridge (*Haematortyx sanguiniceps*)
Crestless Fireback Pheasant (*Lophura erythrophthalma*)
Crested Fireback Pheasant (*L. ignita*)
Bulwer's Pheasant (*L. bulweri*)
Great Argus Pheasant (*Argusianus argus*)
gulls and waders (Charadriiformes)
Common Sandpiper (*Actitis hypoleucos*)

PIGEONS & DOVES (Columbiformes)
Large Green Pigeon (*Treron capellei*)
Thick-billed Green Pigeon (*T. curvirostra*)
Jambu Fruit Pigeon (*Ptilinopus jambu*)
Green Imperial Pigeon (*Ducula aenea*)
Mountain Imperial Pigeon (*D. badia*)

Little Cuckoo Dove (*Macrocygia ruficeps*)
Emerald Dove (*Chalcophaps indica*)

PARROTS (Psittaciformes)
Malay Lorikeet (*Loriculus galqulus*)

CUCKOOS (Cucliformes)
Large Hawk Cuckoo (*Cuculus sparverioides*)
Malayan Hawk Cuckoo (*C. fugax*)
Moustached (Lesser) Hawk Cuckoo (*C. vagans*)
Indian Cuckoo (*C. micropterus*)
Oriental Cuckoo (*C. saturatus*)
Banded Bay Cuckoo (*Cacomantis sonneratii*)
Fan-tailed Cuckoo (*C. variolosus*)
Drongo Cuckoo (*Surniculus lugubris*)
Lesser Green-billed Malcoha (*Phaen coposeus dlardi*)
Raffles' Malcoha (*P. chlorophaeus*)
Rufous-bellied Malcoha (*P. sumatranus*)
Red-billed Malcoha (*P. javanlcus*)
Chestnut-breasted Malcoha (*P. curvirostris*)
Common Coucal (*Centropus sinensis*)
Short-toed Coucal (*C. rectunguis*)
Ground Cuckoo (*Carpococcyx radiceus*)

OWLS (Strigiformes)
Bay Owl (*Phodilus badius*)
Reddish Scops Owl (*Otus rufescens*)
Mountain Scops Owl (*O. spilocephalus*)
(Rajah's) Scops Owl (*O. ?brookei*)
Pigmy owlet (*Glaucidium brodiei*)
Hawk Owl (*Ninox scutulata*)
Malaysian Wood Owl (*Strix leptogrammica*)

NIGHTJARS & ALLIES (Caprimulgiformes)
Large Frogmouth (*Batrachostomus auritus*)
Frogmouth (*Batrachostomus* sp.)

SWIFTS (Apodiformes)
Mossy-nest Swiftlet (*Aerodramus vanikorensis*)
Edible-nest Swiftlet (*A. fuciphagus*)
White-bellied Swiftlet (*Collocalia esculenta*)
White-rumped Spine-tail Swift (*Rhaphidura leucopygialis*)
Malaysian Spine-tailed Swift (*Hirundapus giganteus*)

Crested Tree-swift (*Hemiprocne longipennis*)
White-whiskered Tree-swift (*H. comata*)
trogons (Trogoniformes)
Diard's Trogon (*Harpactes diardi*)
Red-naped Trogon (*H. kasumba*)
Whitehead's Trogon (*H. whiteheadi*)
Scarlet-rumped Trogon (*H. duvauceli*)
Cinnamon-rumped Trogon (*H. orrhophaeus*)
Orange-breasted Trogon (*H. oresdias*)

ROLLERS & ALLIES (Coraciiformes)

Banded Kingfisher (*Lacedo pulchella*)
Chestnut-collared Kingfisher (*Halcyon concreta*)
Black-capped Kingfisher (*H. pileata*)
Stork-billed Kingfisher (*Pelargopsis capensis*)
Deep Blue Kingfisher (*Alcedo meninting*)
Blue-banded Kingfisher (*A. euroyzona*)
Forest Kingfisher (*Ceyx erithacus (rufidorsus)*)
Red-bearded Bee-eater (*Nyceyotnia amictus*)
White-crested Hornbill (*Berenicornis comatus*)
Bushy-crested Hornbill (*Anorrhinus galeritus*)
Wrinkled Hornbill (*Rhyticeros corrugatus*)
Wreathed Hornbill (*R. undulates*)
Black Hornbill (*Anthracoceros malayanus*)
Pied Hornbill (*A. coronatus*)
Rhinceroa Hornbill (*Buceros rhinoceros*)
Helmet Hornbill (*Rhinoplax vigil*)

WOODPECKERS & ALLIES (Piciformes)

Brown Barbet (*Calorhamphus fuliginosua*)
Gold-wiskered Barbet (*Megalaima chrysopogon*)
Many-colored Barbet (*M. rafflesi*)
Gaudy Barbet (*M. mystacophanos*)
Yellow-crowned Barbet (*M. henricii*)
Golden-naped Barbet (*M. pulcherrima*)
Mountain Barbet (*M. monticola*)
Black-throated Barbet (*M. eximia*)
Little Barbet (*M. australis*)
Rufous Piculet (*Sasia abnormia*)
Crimson-winged Woodpecker (*Picus puniceus*)
Checker-throated Woodpecker (*P. mentalia*)
Banded Red Woodpecker (*P. miniacous*)
Rufous Woodpecker (*Celeus brachyurua*)
Fulvous-rumped Barred Woodpecker (*Meiglyptes tristis*)
Buff-necked Barred Wooopecker (*M. takki*)
Grey & Buff Woodpecker (*Hemicircus concretus*)
Olive-backed Three-toed Woodpecker (*Dinopium rafflesi*)

Great Slaty Woodpecker (*Muelleripicus pulverulentus*)
Maroon Woodpecker (*Blythipicus rubiginosus*)
Orange-backed Woodpecker (*Rheinwardtipicus validus*)

PASSERINE BIRDS (Passeres)

Green Broadbill (*Calyptomena viridis*)
Hose's Broadbill (*C. hosei*)
Whitehead's Broadbill (*C. whiteheadi*)
Long-tailed Broadbill (*Psarisomus dalhousiae*)
Black and Red Broadbill (*Cymbirhynchus macrorhynchos*)
Black and Yellow Broadbill (*Eurylaimus ochromalus*)
Banded Broadbill (*E. javanicus*)
Dusky Broadbill (*Corydon sumatranus*)
Blue-banded Pitta (*Pitta arcuata*)
Garnet Pitta (*P. granatina*)
Blue-headed Pitta (*P. baudi*)
Pacific Swallow (*Hirundo tahitica*)
Barn Swallow (*H. rustica*)
Grey Wagtail (*Motacilla caspica*)
Yellow Wagtail (*M. flava*)
Hook-billed Greybird (*Tephrodornis gularis*)
Black-faces Greybird (*Coracina larvata*)
Lesser Greybird (*C. fimbriata*)
Black-winged Flycatcher-Strike (*Hemipus hirundinaceus*)
Bar-winged Flycatcher Strike (*H. picatus*)
Black-breasted Triller (*Chlamybochaera jeffreyi*)
Mountain Minivet (*Pericrocotus solaris*)
Scarlet Minivet (*P. flammeus*)
Green Iora (*Aegithina viridissima*)
Lesser Green Leafbird (*Chloropsis cyanopogon*)
Greater Green Leafbird (*C. sonnerati*)
Blue-winged Leafbird (*C. cochinchinensis*)
Fairy Bluebird (*Irena puella*)
Crested Brown Bulbul (*Pycnonotus eutilotus*)
Black and White Bulbul (*P. melanoleucos*)
Black-headed Bulbul (*P. atriceps*)
Scaly-breasted Bulbul (*P. squamatus*)
Grey-bellied Bulbul (*P. cyaniventris*)
Yellow-crowned Bulbul (*P. zeylanicus*)
Pale-faced Bulbul (*P. flavescens*)
Large Olive Bulbul (*P. plumosus*)
Red-eyed Brown Bulbul (*P. brunneus*)
Cream-vented (White-eyed) Brown Bulbul (*P. simplex*)
Lesser Brown Bulbul (*P. erythropthalmus*)

Scrub (Olive White-throated) Bulbul (*Criniger bres*)

Brown White-throated Bulbul (*C. ochraceus*)

Crestless White-throated Bulbul (*C. phaeocephalus*)

Finsch's Bulbul (*C. finschii*)

Hook-billed Bulbul (*Setornis criniger*)

Hairy-backed Bulbul (*Hypsipetes criniger*)

Streaked Bulbul (*H. malaccensis*)

Crested Olive Bulbul (*H. charlottae*)

Ashy Bulbul (*H. flavala*)

Siberian Blue Robin (*Frithacus cyane*)

Blue Shortwing (*Brachypteryx montana*)

Orange-tailed Shama (*Copsychus pyrropyga*)

Magpie Robin (*C. saularis*)

White-rumped Shama (*C. malabaricus*)

White-crowned Forktail (*Enicurus leschenaulti*)

Chestnut-naped Forktail (*E. ruficapillus*)

Everrett's Ground Thrush (*Zoothera everetii*)

Sunda Whistling Thrush (*Myophoneus glaucinus*)

Rail Babbler (*Eupetes macrocerus*)

Black-capped Jungle Babbler (*Pellorneum capistratum*)

Temmick's Jungle Babbler (*Trichastoma pyrrhogenys*)

Short-tailed Jungle Babbler (*T. malaccense*)

Blyth's Jungle Babbler (*T. rostratum*)

Ferruginous Jungle Babbler (*T. bicolor*)

Horsfield'a Jungle Babbler (*T. aepiarium*)

Greater Red-headed Tree Babbler (*Malacopteron magnum*)

Lesser Red-headed Tree Babbler (*M. cinereum*)

Moustached Babbler (*M. magnirostre*)

White-throated Babbler (*M. albogulare*)

Chestnut-backed Sclmitar Babbler (*Pomatorhinus montanus*)

Bornean Wren Babbler (*Ptilocichla leucogrammica*)

Striped Wren Babbler (*Kenopia striata*)

Black-throated Wren Babbler (*Napothera atrigularis*)

Mountain Wren Babbler (*N. crassa*)

Small Wren Babbler (*N. epilepidota*)

Fluffy-backed Tit Babbler (*Macronus ptilosus*)

Grey-throated Tree Babbler (*Stachyris nigriceps*)

Grey-headed Tree Babbler (*S. poliocephala*)

Black-necked Tree Babbler (*S. nigricollis*)

White-necked Tree Babbler (*S. leucotis*)

Red-rumped Tree Babbler (*S. maculata*)

Red-winged Tree Babbler (*S. erythroptera*)

Hume's Tree Babbler (*S. rufifrons*)

Black Laughing Thrush (*Garrulax lugubris*)

Grey & Brown Laughing Thrush (*G. palliatua*)

Chestnut-capped Laughing Thrush (*G. mitratus*)

Red-winged Shrike Babbler (*Pteruthius flaviscapis*)

Brown Quaker Babbler (*Alcippe brunneicauda*)

Chestnut-headed Minla (*Minla castaneiceps*)

White-bellied Yuhina (*Yuhina zantholeucal*)

Fly eater (*Gerygone sulphurea*)

Short-tailed Bush Warbler (*Cettia whiteheadi*)

Mountain Bush Warbler (*C. fortipes*)

Arctic Leaf Warbler (*Phylloscopus borealis*)

Mountain Leaf Warbler (*P. trivirgatus*)

Yellow-breasted Flycatcher Warbler (*Seicercus montis*)

White-throated Flycatcher W. (*Abroscopus superciliaris*)

Mountain Tailorbird (*Orthotomus cuculatus*)

Ashy (Red-headed) Tailorbird (*O. ruficeps*)

White-throated Fantail (*Rhipidura albicollis*)

Spotted Fantail Flycatcher (*R. perlata*)

Pied Fantail Flycatcher (*R. javanica*)

Grey-headed Flycatcher (*Culicicapa ceylonensis*)

Sooty Flycatcher (*Muscicapa sibirica*)

Brown Flycatcher (*M. latirostris*)

Indigo Flycatcher (*M. indigo*)

Blue and White Flycatcher (*Cyanoptila cyanomelana*)

White-tailed Blue Flycatcher (*Cyornis concreta*)

Pale Blue Flycatcher (*C. unicolor*)

Malaysian Blue Flycatcher (*C. turcosa*)

Large-billed Blue Flycatcher (*C. caerulata*)

Hill Blue Flycatcher (*C. banyumas*)

Bornean Blue Flycatcher (*C. superba*)

White-fronted Blue Flycatcher (*Ficedula hyperythra*)

Orange-breasted Flycatcher (*F. dumetoria*)

Little Pied Flycatcher (*F. westermanni*)

Pigmy Blue Flycatcher (*Muscicapella hodgsoni*)

White-throated Jungle Flycatcher (*Rhinomylas umbratilis*)

Rufous-tailed Jungle Flycatcher (*R. ruficauda*)

White-browed Jungle Flycatcher (*R. gularis*)

Chestnut-winged Monarch Flycatcher (*Philentoma pyrhoterum*)

Maroon-breasted Monarch Flycatcher (*P. velatum*)

Black-naped Blue Monarch Flycatcher (*Hypothymis* azurea)

Paradise Flycatcher (*Terpsiphone paradisi*)

Bornean Mountain Whistler (*Pachycephala hypoxantha*)
Velvet-fronted Nuthatch (*Sitta frontalis*)
Scarlet-breasted Flowerpecker (*Prionochilus thoracicus*)
Yellow-rumped Flowerpecker (*P. xanthopygius*)
Yellow-throated Flowerpecker (*P. maculates*)
Yellow-vented Flowerpecker (*Dicaeum chrysorrheum*)
Black-sided Flowerpecker (*D. monticola*)
Pain-coloured Sunbird (*Anthreptes simplex*)
Rufous-throated Sunbird (*A. rhodolaema*)
Ruby-cheeked Sunbird (*A. singalensis*)
Purple-naped Sunbird (*Hypogramma hypogrammicum*)
Yellow-backed Sunbird (*Aethopyga siparaja*)
Scarlet Sunbird (*A. mystacalis*)

Little Spiderhunter (*Arachnothera longirostra*)
Long-billed Spiderhunter (*A. robusta*)
Grey-breasted Spiderhunter (*A. affinis*)
Whitehead's Spiderhunter (*A. juliae*)
Black-capped White-eye (*Zosterops atricapilla*)
Mountain Blackeye (*Chlorocharis emiliae*)
Grackle or Talking Myna (*Gracuia religiosa*)
Bamboo Munia (*Erythrura hyperythra*)
Crow-billed Drongo (*Dicrurus annectans*)
Grey Drongo (*D. leucophaeus*)
Hair-crested Drongo (*D. hottentottus*)
Large Racket-tailed Drongo (*D. paradiseus*)
Black-headed Oriole (*Oriolus xanthonotus*)
Black and Crimson Oriole (*O. cruentus*)
Crested Jay (*Platylophus galericulatus*)
Malaysian Treepie (*Dendrocitta occipitalis*)
Slender-billed Crow (*Crovus enca*)

262 species

Titles by *Natural History Publications (Borneo)*

For more information, please contact us at

Natural History Publications (Borneo) Sdn. Bhd.
A913, 9th Floor, Phase 1, Wisma Merdeka,
P.O. Box 15566,
88864 Kota Kinabalu, Sabah, Malaysia
Tel: 088-233098 Fax: 088-240768 e-mail: chewlun@tm.net.my
www.nhpborneo.com

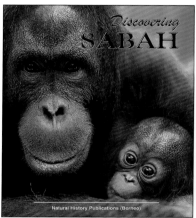

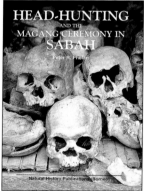

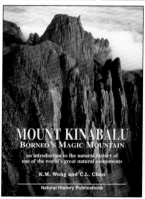
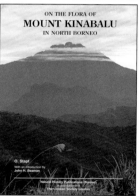

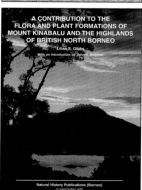
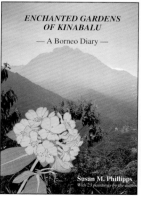

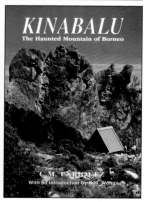

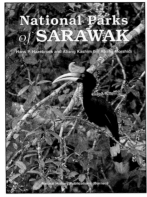

National Parks
of SARAWAK
Hans P. Hazebroek and Abang Kashim bin Abang Morshidi
National History Publications (Borneo)

A Walk through the
LOWLAND RAIN FOREST
of Sabah
Elaine J.F. Campbell

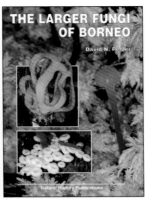

THE LARGER FUNGI
OF BORNEO
David N. Pegler
Natural History Publications

RAFFLESIA
OF THE WORLD
JAMILI NAIS

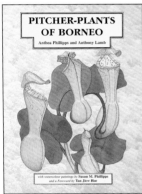

PITCHER-PLANTS
OF BORNEO
Anthea Phillipps and Anthony Lamb
with watercolour paintings by Susan M. Phillipps
and a Foreword by Tan Jiew Hoe

A GUIDE TO THE
Pitcher Plants
of Sabah
Charles Clarke
Natural History Publications (Borneo)

A GUIDE TO THE
Pitcher Plants of
Peninsular Malaysia
Charles Clarke
Natural History Publications (Borneo)

NEPENTHES
of BORNEO
CHARLES CLARKE
Natural History Publications

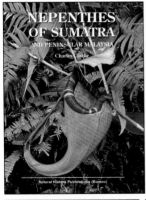

NEPENTHES
OF SUMATRA
AND PENINSULAR MALAYSIA
Charles Clarke
Natural History Publications (Borneo)

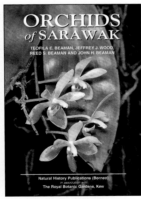

ORCHIDS
of SARAWAK
TEOFILA E. BEAMAN, JEFFREY J. WOOD,
REED S. BEAMAN AND JOHN H. BEAMAN
Natural History Publications (Borneo)
in association with
The Royal Botanic Gardens, Kew

ORCHIDS
of SUMATRA
J.B. Comber
Natural History Publications (Borneo)
in association with
The Royal Botanic Gardens, Kew

DENDROCHILUM
OF BORNEO
Jeffrey J. Wood
Natural History Publications (Borneo)
in association with
The Royal Botanic Gardens, Kew

THE PLANTS of
MOUNT KINABALU
3. GYMNOSPERMS AND NON-ORCHID MONOCOTYLEDONS
John H. Beaman and Reed S. Beaman
Natural History Publications (Borneo)
in association with
The Royal Botanic Gardens, Kew

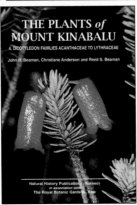

THE PLANTS of
MOUNT KINABALU
4. DICOTYLEDON FAMILIES ACANTHACEAE TO LYTHRACEAE
John H. Beaman, Christiane Anderson and Reed S. Beaman
Natural History Publications (Borneo)
in association with
The Royal Botanic Gardens, Kew

The Genus
PAPHIOPEDILUM
Second Edition
Phillip Cribb
Natural History Publications (Borneo)
in association with
The Royal Botanic Gardens, Kew

SLIPPER ORCHIDS
OF BORNEO
Phillip Cribb
Natural History Publications

THE GENUS
COELOGYNE
A SYNOPSIS

Dudley Clayton

Natural History Publications (Borneo)
in association with
The Royal Botanic Gardens, Kew

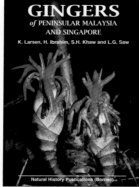

GINGERS
of PENINSULAR MALAYSIA
AND SINGAPORE

K. Larsen, H. Ibrahim, S.H. Khaw and L.G. Saw

Natural History Publications (Borneo)

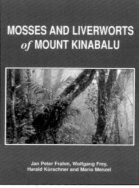

MOSSES AND LIVERWORTS
of MOUNT KINABALU

Jan Peter Frahm, Wolfgang Frey,
Harald Kürschner and Mario Menzel

IN BRUNEI FORESTS
An Introduction to the Plant Life of Brunei Darussalam

K.M. Wong
with watercolours by C.L. Chan

A Revised Edition

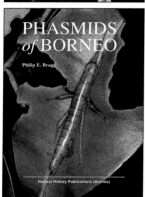

PHASMIDS
of BORNEO

Philip E. Bragg

Natural History Publications (Borneo)

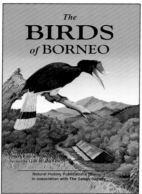

The
BIRDS
of BORNEO

Fourth Edition
Revised by G.W.H. Davison

Natural History Publications (Borneo)
in association with The Sabah Society

The
BIRDS
of BURMA

Fourth Edition
Bertram E. Smythies

Natural History Publications (Borneo)

Swiftlets of Borneo
BUILDERS OF EDIBLE NESTS
Lim Chan Koon and Earl of Cranbrook

Natural History Publications (Borneo)

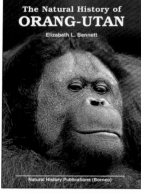

The Natural History of
ORANG-UTAN

Elizabeth L. Bennett

Natural History Publications (Borneo)

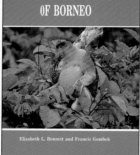

PROBOSCIS MONKEYS
OF BORNEO

Elizabeth L. Bennett and Francis Gombek

A Field Guide to the
FROGS OF BORNEO

Robert F. Inger
Robert B. Stuebing

The Natural History of
AMPHIBIANS AND REPTILES
IN SABAH

Robert F. Inger and Tan Fui Lian

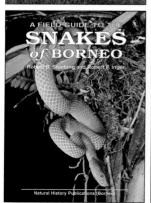

A FIELD GUIDE TO THE
SNAKES
of BORNEO

Robert B. Stuebing and Robert F. Inger

Natural History Publications (Borneo)

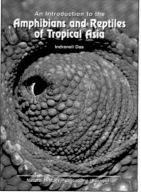

An Introduction to the
Amphibians and Reptiles
of Tropical Asia
Indraneil Das

Natural History Publications (Borneo)

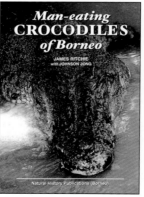

Man-eating
CROCODILES
of Borneo

JAMES RITCHIE
with JOHNSON JONG

Natural History Publications (Borneo)

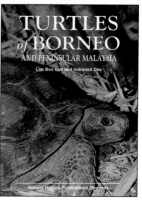

TURTLES
of BORNEO
AND PENINSULAR MALAYSIA

Lim Boo Liat and Indraneil Das

Natural History Publications (Borneo)

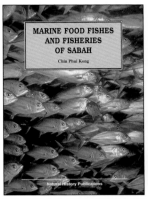

MARINE FOOD FISHES
AND FISHERIES
OF SABAH

Chin Phui Kong

Natural History Publications

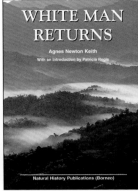

WHITE MAN
RETURNS

Agnes Newton Keith

With an Introduction by Patricia Regis

Natural History Publications (Borneo)

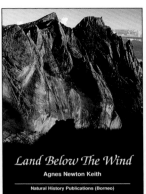

Land Below The Wind

Agnes Newton Keith

Natural History Publications (Borneo)

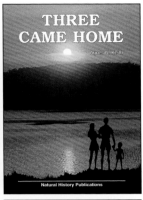

THREE
CAME HOME

Agnes Newton Keith

Natural History Publications

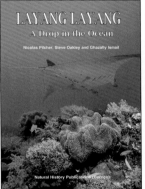

LAYANG LAYANG
A Drop in the Ocean

Nicolas Pilcher, Steve Oakley and Ghazally Ismail

Natural History Publications (Borneo)

WITH THE WILD MEN OF
BORNEO

Elizabeth Mershon

Natural History Publications (Borneo)

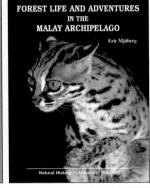

FOREST LIFE AND ADVENTURES
IN THE
MALAY ARCHIPELAGO

Eric Mjöberg

Natural History Publications (Borneo)

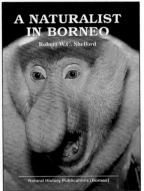

A NATURALIST
IN BORNEO

Robert W.C. Shelford

Natural History Publications (Borneo)

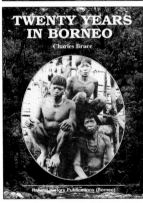

TWENTY YEARS
IN BORNEO

Charles Bruce

Natural History Publications (Borneo)

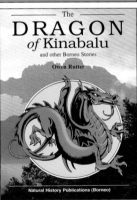

The
DRAGON
of Kinabalu
and other Borneo Stories

Owen Rutter

Natural History Publications (Borneo)

A CULTURAL HERITAGE OF NORTH BORNEO
Animal Tales
of Sabah

P. S. Shim

with illustrations by Yong Ket Hyon

Natural History Publications (Borneo)

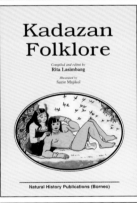

Kadazan
Folklore

Compiled and edited by
Rita Lasimbang

Illustrated by
Suzie Majikol

Natural History Publications (Borneo)

AN INTRODUCTION TO THE
TRADITIONAL COSTUMES
of SABAH

edited by
Rita Lasimbang and Stella Moo-Tan

Manual Latihan
Pemuliharaan dan Penyelidikan
Hidupan Liar di Lapangan

Alan Rabinowitz
Diterjemah oleh
Maryati Mohamed

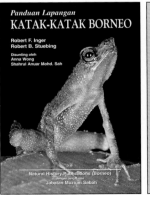

Panduan Lapangan
KATAK-KATAK BORNEO

Robert F. Inger
Robert B. Stuebing

Disunting oleh
Anna Wong
Shahrul Anuar Mohd. Sah

Natural History Publications (Borneo)
dengan kerjasama
Jabatan Muzium Sabah

Etnobotani

GARY J. MARTIN
Diterjemah oleh Maryati Mohamed

PEOPLE
Plants

SEBUAH MANUAL PEMULIHARAAN
'MANUSIA DAN TUMBUHAN'

Natural History Publications (Borneo)